POWER MUDRAS - New Edition by SABRINA MESKO

BY SABRINA MESKO

HEALING MUDRAS
Yoga for Your Hands
Random House - Original edition

POWER MUDRAS
Yoga Hand Postures for Women
Random House - Original edition

MUDRA - GESTURES OF POWER
DVD - Sounds True

CHAKRA MUDRAS DVD set
HAND YOGA for Vitality, Creativity and Success
HAND YOGA for Concentration, Love and Longevity

HEALING MUDRAS
Yoga for Your Hands - New Edition

HEALING MUDRAS - New Edition in full color:
Healing Mudras I. ~ For Your Body
Healing Mudras II. ~ For Your Mind
Healing Mudras III. ~ For Your Soul

POWER MUDRAS
Yoga Hand Postures for Women - New Edition

MUDRA THERAPY
Hand Yoga for Pain Management and Conquering Illness

YOGA MIND
45 Meditations for Inner Peace, Prosperity and Protection

MUDRAS FOR ASTROLOGICAL SIGNS
Volumes I. ~ XII.
MUDRAS FOR ARIES, TAURUS, GEMINI, CANCER, LEO, VIRGO, LIBRA, SCORPIO, SAGITTARIUS, CAPRICORN, AQUARIUS, PISCES
12 Book Series

LOVE MUDRAS
Hand Yoga for Two

MUDRAS AND CRYSTALS
The Alchemy of Energy protection

POWER
MUDRAS

Yoga Hand Postures for WOMEN

By Sabrina Mesko Ph.D.H.

The material contained in this book has been written for informational
purposes and is not intended as a substitute for medical advice
nor is it intended to diagnose, treat, cure, or prevent disease.
If you have a medical issue or illness, consult a qualified physician.

A Mudra Hands™ Book
Published by Mudra Hands Publishing

Imprint of
Arnica Press
www.ArnicaPress.com

Copyright © 2002, 2013 Sabrina Mesko Ph.D.H.

Photography by Mara, Kiar Mesko, Michael Wacht
Stone sculpture and illustrations by Kiar Mesko
Cover photo by Kiar Mesko
On the Cover - Mudra of Divine Worship

Nature photography shot in Malibu, California,
and the Triglav National Park in Slovenian Alps
Printed in the United States of America

ISBN-13: 978-0615943282
ISBN-10: 0615943284

Originally published by Random House in 2002
Under the title Power Mudras-*Yoga Hand Postures for Women*
New, revised, updated and expanded

For my Magnificent Mother

and all the Loving,

Courageous,

Compassionate,

Empowered,

Enlightened,

Generous,

Giving,

Healing,

Nurturing,

Selfless,

and Wise

Women of the World...

CONTENTS

THE MUDRA PRACTICE IS A COMPLIMENTARY HEALING TECHNIQUE,
THAT OFFERS FAST AND EFFECTIVE POSITIVE RESULTS.

MUDRAS WORK HARMONIOUSLY WITH OTHER TRADITIONAL,
ALTERNATIVE AND COMPLEMENTARY HEALING PROTOCOLS.

THEY HELP RESTORE DEPLETED SUBTLE ENERGY STATES
AND OPTIMIZE THE PRACTITIONER'S
OVERALL STATE OF WELLNESS.

INTRODUCTION

The great news is that despite many circumstances for a healthy lifestyle changing over the years, what has not changed are the powerful benefits you can receive from the practice of the wonderful ancient Mudra–hand yoga techniques. Mudras work in all environments under any circumstances, and are truly time-resilient.

It has been an absolute joy to hear from my readers thru the years and witness how many of you have embraced and benefited from the Mudra practice. Since the first publication of "Power Mudras" over ten years ago, I have further developed the use of Mudra Therapy specifically when conquering various ailments. Mudras are exceptionally effective for the process of whole body regeneration and elimination of toxins. I continue to be fascinated, humbled, and immersed in them.

May this book remind you once again that there is nothing as beneficial, wonderful, and important as giving yourself some solitude to find and establish your inner peace. Once that is achieved, your life changes. No matter what is happening around you, the gift of calmness, strength, focus, and serenity is yours.

Life is a wild journey, nothing is everlasting, it is a kaleidoscope of moments; some glorious, some tragic, some dream-like amazing, and others you wish wouldn't have happened. But you cannot control every element of your life.

As women we have a profound need to nurture, care for, and fix everything. We are also pressured to show tremendous strength, ability to do it all- and that is simply impossible. You can do a lot, and from the outside it may look like you are doing it all, but there are always elements that will be compromised and only you know about them.

The question is, are you happy? Are you doing what you want? Are you trying to fit into a mold, fulfill everyone's expectation, change yourself a million times to suit others? Are you content with who you are, what you've become, choices you've made? Are you fulfilled or still searching for answers to your happiness outside of yourself? That is a difficult one.
Slow down, take a moment, and be honest with yourself.
Yes, you must do that. Why?

Because only you have all the answers to your questions, only you know what you truly, deeply want, and only you can give yourself what you need. The longer you avoid facing this truth, the longer you will stumble around seeking, disappointed, perhaps even bitter that things did not go your way. Things go the way you navigate thru life, according to your circumstances and your choices. Paying attention to your inner thoughts and needs is one of those very important choices.

It is also a choice that you take time, know yourself, find absolute peace with your past, and it is your choice to be happy with who you have become. It is a choice. The sooner you claim it, the faster you will find that inner peace.

Life's accomplishments are measured by a whole set of different factors than it may seem. It is not about what you surround yourself with materially, it is about what is inside you and the environment you create around yourself no matter where, how and with whom you are spending your life. An easy ride is not the purpose of life. A life full of challenges that you managed to overcome, that is your wealth-your experiences, therein lies the secret.

Why? Because you character is tested, choices are presented, decisions are made, and your behavior and disposition reveal who you really are. You learn, you experience, your soul becomes wiser and wealthier. It may seem strange, but that is how it is.

Women certainly face different challenges than men and I believe being a man holds plenty of challenges as well. The saying that this is a man's world holds weight, however I am optimistic that women are breaking that glass ceiling as well. Being a woman in this life, I still make an effort to understand how challenging it is to be a man. However, obviously it is easier for me to relate in depth to a woman's life. As we all age every singular minute of the day, may I suggest you embrace time and be grateful that you gained experiences, hopefully becoming wiser with each adventure.

That is how I look at it. Understandably with time, a few wrinkles are gained as well. Now you have a choice-do you select to fight them with desperation, chasing after someone you were twenty years ago, or do you make friends with time and enjoy the changes.

My life has been very interesting in that department. I grew up incredibly fast having been enrolled into a professional ballet school at age three. By age fourteen, I was a professional classical ballerina dancing in the opera house. From there my life moved fast and furious as one would say, through a million experiences, and the funny thing was, I was always the youngest everywhere. The youngest dancer in numerous companies, later Broadway and TV shows and so on. With my life packed with colorful experiences I embraced each year with curiosity and much enthusiasm, for I am the eternal optimist. The funny thing is that to this day, I often find myself surrounded by women that are much older and I find it a privilege to be able to see life thru their eyes and hear about their experiences when life truly was incredibly different for women. Things change with time, that is certain.

Now, what seems like lifetimes away from my ballet years, I am still relatively young, even though sometimes I feel thousands of years old, but not in a physical way. I feel perpetually youthful. That will never change in my mind.

So what is age really about? It is about how one feels and thinks. For women this is a very important element. Why? Because our current culture is preoccupied with eternal youth, being thin, and comparing ourselves to a completely airbrushed photograph we see in an advertisement. Comparing yourself to a celebrity who seemingly loses all baby weight in a week is of course completely disruptive and unrealistic. Even if it all seems rosy for that particular celebrity, believe me, she is still a human being with tons of crazy pressure, and odd circumstances hard to escape. The illusions created are expensive, stressful and fleeting.

So if you are aware of those elements you will hopefully eliminate the silly habit of comparing yourself to anyone else. I remind you of this because we live in a celebrity and social media driven society and virtual world where our only way of communicating seems to be online, and we do not really see an "ideal example" in person.

The whole world seems to be informed in an instant simultaneously of an event and even though I am all for this super highway of communication, oddly enough it also creates a narrower communication path. We spend less time actually conversing in person, observing the world and people around us in "real life", and consequentially we are more and more detached from reality. So we function in a different "reality". That of course then becomes a distorted reality- a fantasy of some sort.

Another important aspect to know is that anyone, and I mean truly anyone can look amazingly beautiful between ages nineteen to twenty-five. That is the usual age limit where you can do anything and still look amazing. By anything I mean, eat unhealthy, sleep zero and wonder around without a real goal. And then, the consequences of this lifestyle start showing up. The deep unhappiness or unhealthy lifestyle will eventually show, but most certainly after age forty, there will be a large difference. And after age fifty, there is absolutely no more hiding. Your facial expression will reveal how you feel inside and your unhappiness will burst out. No stopping there. So what does that mean?

It means you need to start taking care of yourself now. Begin facing the "real you" sooner rather than later-the " inner you" that is a bright, lovely spark of Divine light and longs to be given a chance to shine brightly, and enlighten those around you. Give yourself the gift of being still for a moment and truly honestly reflect who you are, where you are, what are you doing, and where are you going. You have all the answers to all your questions so please, listen. If something is not good for you, you know it deep inside. Can you pay attention to that inner voice and really hear it? It is your higher self, giving you clear navigation where you should turn and what you should do. But if your mind is too noisy you will not hear anything but the noise.

In this book you will find countless Mudra combinations that are very specific for your needs, with the purpose of reclaiming your power, finding a perfect balance in your life, and maintaining that eternal youthful appearance.

Time does not matter, age does not matter, what matters is how you feel, inside and out. Take your power into your hands and remember: when you are happy, everyone else around you will be and you will be a better daughter, girlfriend, mother, wife, sister, grandmother, woman and a teacher to all. And most importantly, please remember, it is absolutely never too late to start. Begin today and be the woman you always wanted to be; beautiful beyond measure, powerful like the Sun, and wise beyond imagination. Reclaim your power, you are on your way!

Blessings now and always,

Sabrina

MUDRA INDEX

WHAT IS A MUDRA?

A Mudra is an ancient healing hand gesture, a yoga hand pose, a symbolic gesture or hand position, a basic element of dance ritual, and an integral part of religious ceremonies. Mudras date back thousands of years and are a part of every culture on earth. The language of hand gestures knows no barriers of place and time.

Ritual hand gestures originated in Egypt about five thousand years ago and got the name Mudra when they became and intricate part of yoga practice in India. Almost identical Mudras can be found in religious sculptures of Europe, India, Asia, North and South America, and Egypt.

We use Mudras every day of our lives. Notice how you hold your hands during various times of the day. Are our palms open, so that you're open to new energies? Or are you clenching your fists and keeping suppressed energy locked within? Maybe you place your hand on your chest when dealing with matters of the deep emotion-using the healing power of your own hands to soothe the pain in your heart.

In this book you will discover the hidden meaning and power within each Mudra pose. Some Mudras will feel more comfortable than other and you may be especially attracted to a certain Mudra. Listen to your intuition and explore the various effects that Mudra practice offers. Mudras can help you heal, rejuvenate, and balance your body, mind, and spirit, and connect you to the voice of divine wisdom. Most of all, Mudras will awaken and magnify your inner power.

YOUR ENERGY BODY - AURA

Your body is an amazing structure of electromagnetic energy vibrations. Your aura, or the energy field around your body, is very receptive and sensitive to the vibrations of your environment. Sound, color, light, emotions (your own and other people's), animals, food, and all of nature affect your energy field. When you are in a happy environment, filled with love and surrounded by your favorite music, colors, and harmonious people, your aura expands and glows stronger. If you find yourself in a dangerous or uncomfortable situation, or you feel hurt or angry, your aura will instantly reflect a more contained and protective energy field.

CHAKRAS

Along your spine are located seven major energy centers called chakras. They are spinning in a clockwise direction and are connected to and affect your entire physical, emotional, and spiritual well-being. To understand the connection between bodies' physical organs and our chakras, it is important that we are familiar with the chakras' basic functions and what empowers and affects them.

FIRST CHAKRA

Is located at the base of the spine and affects the function of the gonad glands. This chakra corresponds with your feelings about survival, financial security, vitality, and foundation. The color that affects it is red. To empower your feelings of inner security and vitality, practice First Chakra Mudras and combine different healing elements of your choice.

THE HEALING ELEMENTS OF NATURE

SOUND
Listen to the sound of singing and chirping birds
FLOWERS
Surround yourself with red roses, tulips, dahlias, and carnations
FRUIT
Red apples, cherries, strawberries, red plums, and raspberries

SECOND CHAKRA

Is located in the area of sex organs and affects the function of the adrenal glands. This chakra is connected to your sexual expression, creativity, procreation, and family. The color that affects it is orange. To energize your sexuality and creativity, practice the Second Chakra Mudras and combine different healing elements of your choice.

THE HEALING ELEMENTS OF NATURE

SOUND
Listen to the sound of streams or waterfalls
FLOWERS
Enjoy the sight of orange roses, tulips, and gladiolas
FRUIT
Oranges, apricots, tangerines, mangoes, and papayas

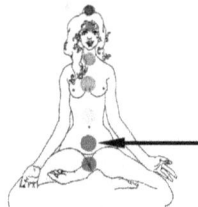

THIRD CHAKRA

Is located in the area of the solar plexus and affects the function of the pancreas gland. This chakra corresponds to your ego, intellect, and the mind, and is a strong emotional center. Feelings of anger and fear tend to gather in this center. Its empowering color is yellow. When you need to stimulate the brain, diminish fears, and resolve and let go of anger, practice the Third Chakra Mudras and combine different healing elements of your choice.

THE HEALING ELEMENTS OF NATURE

SOUND
Listen to the sound of crackling fire

FLOWERS
Surround yourself with yellow daffodils, sunflowers, narcissi, and primroses

FRUIT
Yellow grapes, lemons, grapefruit, bananas, and pineapples

FOURTH CHAKRA

Is located in the area of the heart and is connected to the function of the thymus gland. This chakra corresponds to all matters of the heart, love, self-love, compassion, and faith. The healing color for this center is green. To soothe your broken heart and open yourself to the new experiences, practice the Fourth Chakra Mudras and combine different healing elements of your choice.

THE HEALING ELEMENTS OF NATURE

SOUND
Listen to the sound of wind
FLOWERS
Gaze upon green grass, trees, and evergreens
FRUIT
Green apples, pears, and kiwi

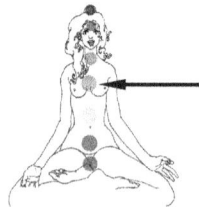

FIFTH CHAKRA

Is located in the area of the throat and affects the function of the thyroid gland. This chakra represents all matters of communication, truth, higher knowledge, and your voice. Its healing color is blue. To clear and empower your communication ability and release unspoken words of truth, practice the Fifth Chakra Mudras and combine different healing elements of your choice.

THE HEALING ELEMENTS OF NATURE

SOUND
Listen to the sound of the ocean

FLOWERS
Enjoy the sight of iris, hyacinths, and bluebells

FRUIT
Blueberries, blue grapes, and blue plums

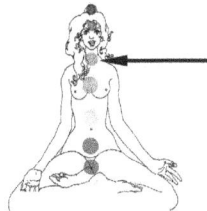

SIXTH CHAKRA

Is located in the area of the Third Eye and affects the function of the pineal gland. This chakra is our connection to intuition, inner vision, and the Third Eye. Its healing color is indigo. For magnifying the intuitive guiding powers and deeper spiritual experiences, practice the Sixth Chakra Mudras and combine different healing elements of your choice.

THE HEALING ELEMENTS OF NATURE

SOUND
Listen to the sound of all life and the universe, the sound of silence

FLOWERS
Enjoy the beauty of Spanish lavender, lilacs, and orchids

FRUIT
Dark grapes, blackberries, and black cherries

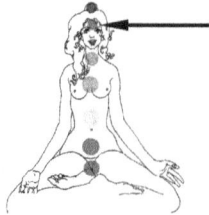

SEVENTH CHAKRA

Is located in the crown of the head and affects the pituitary gland. This chakra is our connection to the universal God consciousness and the heavens. Its healing color is violet or white. To elevate your spirit and get rid of negative or heavy feelings, practice the Seventh Chakra Mudras and combine different healing elements of your choice.

THE HEALING ELEMENTS OF NATURE

SOUND
Listen to the sound of your breath

FLOWERS
Enjoy white roses, magnolias, camellias, daisies, and lilies of the valley

FRUIT
Pale honeydew melons, and pale grapefruits

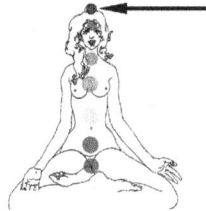

Chakras in Your Palms

Besides the seven chakras that run along your spine, you also have a chakra in each foot and in each palm.

The chakras in your feet are your receptors for feeling grounded and connected to Mother Earth. Walking barefoot in the grass or on the beach will instantly reconnect you with the healing power of nature and help revitalize your body.

Your hands are sensitive to all of nature's elements that help stimulate energy. Place your hands under running water and you will immediately feel refreshed. Go to the garden and touch the earth. As you hold it in your palms and feel its texture, let its nourishing energy permeate your hands. Touch a delicate flower. Feel the gentle tenderness of the bloom. Hold or caress a pet and instantly feel love, peace, and tranquility.

The chakras in your hands relate to giving and receiving. Pay attention to who you shake hands with and what you touch. A gentle daily hand massage will stimulate all reflex areas in your hands and bring you great benefits.

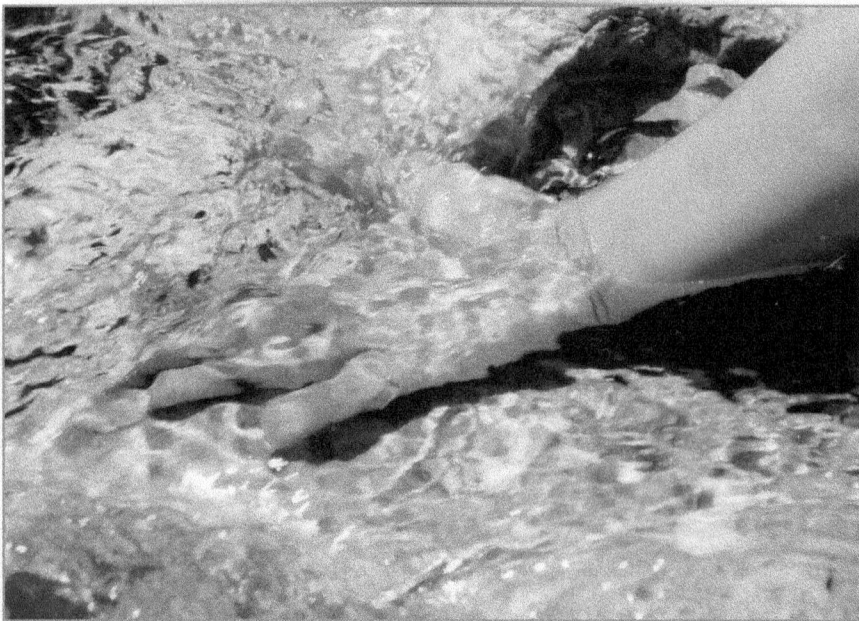

Nadis

Your body has a network of seventy-two thousand electric currents called nadis. They run throughout your body from your toes to the top of your head and out to your fingertips. These channels of energy must be clear and vibrant with life force for your optimum health and empowerment.

Your aura expands beyond your physical body and within this energy field are other subtle chakras. The layers of finer energy vibrations that surround your body each reflect a certain aspect of your soul's vibration. Some health problems exist in your field of energy frequency long before they actually manifest in your physical body. Often an emotionally negative cluster of energy manifests into a physical cluster of negative energy or disease. It is very important to pay attention and balance your emotional and mental states as they reflect and affect your physical body. Your mental or emotional state projects onto and affects your physical body. Dealing with your emotions and your psyche is essential for maintaining vibrant, balanced, and healthy energy vibration.

Your thinking patters are also a great contributor to your overall state of health. Conscious positive affirmations can redirect your mindset towards optimal health.

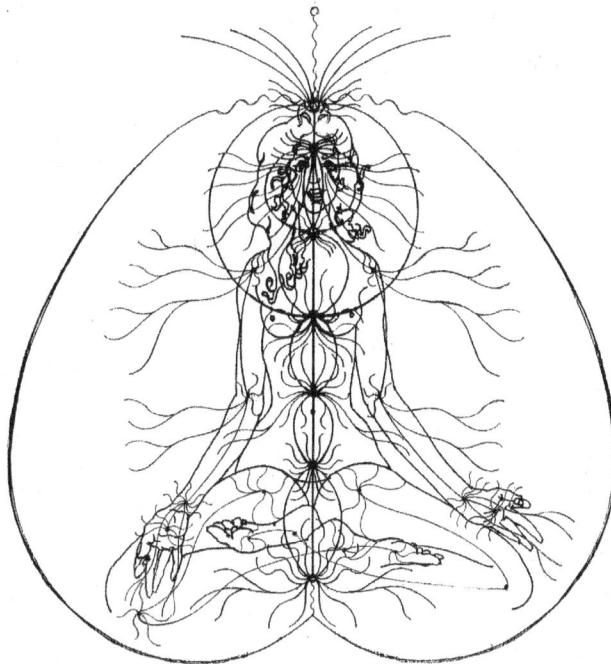

Chakras and Nadis in Your Body

Your Body, Hands and the Cosmos

The right side of the body is ruled by the Sun. It reflects the male qualities of your personality and is connected to your father. The left side of your body is ruled by the Moon, reflects the feminine side of your personality, and is connected to your mother. With the practice of Mudras you are reconnecting the nadis of masculine and feminine qualities and energies and creating a balance and harmony within the physical, emotional, and mental aspects of your being. During the Mudra practice you are also magnifying the effects of the solar system on your physical body. Each finger is specifically influenced by the following planets:

The THUMB - Mars -
WILLPOWER, LOGIC, EGO

The INDEX finger - Jupiter -
KNOWLEDGE, JUSTICE, TRUTH, HONOR, SELF-CONFIDENCE

The MIDDLE finger - Saturn -
PATIENCE, EMOTIONAL CONTROL, AMBITION

The RING finger -Sun -
VITALITY, HEALTH, MATTERS OF THE HEART

The LITTLE finger - Mercury -
SPOKEN AND WRITTEN COMMUNICATION, BEAUTY, CREATIVITY

Instructions for Practice

How do Mudras Work?

During your Mudra practice you are connecting your fingertips, palms, and hands in specific ways that help you activate, redirect, and recharge the energy in your entire being. Accessing your chakra centers and your open nadis magnifies and empowers your body's energy; your emotional state is affected in a positive self-empowering way; your mental state is greatly improved; and your physical body becomes revitalized and full of energy. Mudras have a powerful healing effect on your spiritual state as you become more in tune and connected to the universal wisdom. Mudras are an ideal preventative technique and are excellent for maintaining a healthy body, mind, and soul. Daily practice will help you release old, draining, unhealthy energies, and will recharge you with new, vibrant life force.

YOUR TIME AND PLACE FOR MUDRA PRACTICE

Mudras can be practiced anyplace and anytime you can find a few minutes to yourself. It is preferable to find a quiet and peaceful place where no one can disturb you. When you are new to Mudras it is important that you can fully feel the effects without any distractions. Proper breathing is essential and should be practiced in a quiet environment so that you can hear yourself.

Once you've become familiar with the practice, you can practice Mudras in any environment. Mudras are very helpful in a variety of situations when you need quick help in a matter of minutes. Practice the Mudras before and during any challenging situation: a hectic day at home, an exam, a demanding meeting at work, a visit to a doctor's or dentist's office, when you are stressed, impatient, in need of guidance, or in pain, and in many more instances.

Mudras should not be practiced on a full stomach. Wait at least an hour after a big meal. Make a habit of practicing the Mudras first thing in the morning to begin your day. A great time for practice is also in the evening before retiring, for a restful and rejuvenating sleep. For an extended practice, wrap a shawl around your shoulders and body. It is normal for your body temperature to drop slightly during Mudra and meditation practice.

THE VARIOUS STAGES OF MUDRA PRACTICE

MUDRA POSTURE

Sit in a comfortable position with a straight back and relax your shoulders and neck. You can sit cross-legged in a lotus position or in a chair. If sitting, both feet are placed parallel and with equal weight on the ground. Sitting is preferable, but Mudra practice is beneficial even while you are standing or lying down.

Your eyes are an important part of your practice. They may remain half-open and focused gently over the tip of your nose, or you may close your eyes and gently direct them toward the area of the Third Eye. If you wish to keep your eyes open, relax the eyelids and direct your eyes into the middle distance. Never force your eyes into an uncomfortable or painful position. After adjusting your posture and your eyes, place your hands in the Mudra position and begin.

BREATH CONTROL

Proper breathing is essential for your health and magnifies the power of your Mudra practice. Inhale and exhale only through the nose unless otherwise specified. Your breathing should be deep, slow, and calm, centered at the solar plexus area. Avoid lifting the shoulders and breathing from the upper chest area. When you inhale, your solar plexus should expand, and when you exhale, it should contract. This breathing techniques is also very helpful when you suffer from asthma, anxiety, or pain. Focusing your breath on the stomach area will help alleviate stress, fear, anger, and many other negative emotions you may hold there. Therefore concentrate and deeply inhale and exhale, releasing toxins and making space for new, positive energy.

In addition to this deep, long breathing, Mudras sometimes require a technique called the breath fire. It works under the same principles, from the solar plexus area, but at a faster pace. In this case you place the emphasis on the exhalation and each breath lasts about a second. It is important that you master the deep, long breathing first and then slowly increase the speed of your breathing to the breath of fire. When you're starting out, practice the breath of fire for a short time and then return to the deep, long breath. Avoid practicing the breath of fire during the heavy days of your period. The breath of fire energizes and stimulates your body, whereas the deep, long breathing calms and relaxes you. Both breathing techniques clear your body of toxins, help you stay healthy and energized, and give you glowing, radiant skin and a youthful glow.

WITHDRAWAL AND CONCENTRATION

Close your eyes, forget the environment, and go within. This is the moment in which you learn to enjoy stillness. Become at peace with yourself and remove yourself from the environment - with your mind. Listen only to your breath and let all other sounds come and go without disturbing you.

Firmly hold your mind on a specific desired topic. Direct your closed eyes towards your Third Eye area. Gently look slightly upward and look far into the distance. That is your focus point where you can penetrate through the darkness and open the window into infinity. If you need an answer to a specific question, ask your Higher consciousness to provide your with an answer. Know that only a clear question can get a clear answer. Do not doubt or overanalyze the answer. If you receive no answer, let go, and know that in due time your question will be answered.

MEDITATION

This is the time when you become still, free your mind, and expand your awareness beyond limitations. Meditation has many healing effects on your entire being. Clinical research has shown that regular meditation successfully and positively affects your capacity to concentrate, improves circulation, lowers high blood pressure, releases stress, improves your nerves, helps with depression, migraine headaches, insomnia, and addictions, and improves the overall immune system. Allow yourself to just be. Let your Higher self open up and commune with the Divine. Become one with the Universe.

VISUALIZATION

Your mind is an extremely powerful instrument. With the practice of Mudras and meditation you will learn to quiet your mind. You can practice visualization to help still and focus the mind. You can visualize in your mind a healthy state of your body, a positive situation, or a good outcome of an event. Visualization is like a rehearsal in your mind of something positive that you desire to accomplish. If you can see yourself succeeding, you have actually made it a reality in your mind and you are going to feel more prepared and self-confident when you find yourself in the actual situation. In our mind the event is possible, it already happened and you did well. You must be able to see it in your mind first. For example, a professional athlete might visualize himself physically accomplishing a perfect routine in his mind. That will greatly improve his chances of succeeding when the time comes for him to actually perform. Certainly a great amount of physical training will be essential, but the mind has to be in as great a shape as the physical body.

When dealing with a health challenge you will speed your recovery if you visualize yourself in a healthy and vibrant state, having overcome the ailment. By visualizing a calming and healing environment, you can transform your well-being, reduce stress, and improve your overall health. Visualization is equally important when you want to attract abundance. Seeing yourself as successful first in your mind is followed by you attracting circumstances and people who will help you succeed.

Visualization is very easy and can be practiced anywhere. During your practice of Mudras is an excellent time to visualize the desired outcome. For example, when practicing the Mudra for protecting your health, visualize your body surrounded by white healing energy filling your with light. Create a healthy imprint of yourself.

AFFIRMATION AND PRAYER

Affirmations are a great technique to direct your mind power in the positive self-healing direction of our choice. You decide what thinking pattern you would like to have, and then repeat those words in your mind. The inner voice definitely affects how you perceive and present yourself to the world and live your life. It is essential for your health, happiness, and success to pay attention to how you think and what you hear in your mind.

Listen well and notice what you hear in that inner conversation. Is it and old scolding you heard as a child that followed you to this day and had prevented you from being your best? Is it an encouraging voice that helps you pull thru everything in life and survive trials and tribulations with power and resilience?

Choose to have a positive outlook on life, give yourself a well-deserved pat on the back, and enjoy life's adventures. Affirmations are essential when you want to take your destiny into your own hands. When you are practicing Mudras you can magnify the desired effects by repeating the suggested affirmation. During the practice your mind is open and receptive to new information. If you consciously choose a positive affirmation as your inner conversation, you are well on your way to reprogramming your mind to become a positive, self-loving, encouraging, and a supportive ally in your life's adventures.

If you prefer, you may enrich your Mudra practice with a personal prayer. By repeating the prayer in your mind during the practice you will engrave it in your subconsciousness so that is may help, protect, and carry you through challenging times.

MANTRA

You can utilize the healing power of sound vibrations when you add the element of mantras into your practice. The hard palate on your mouth has fifty-eight energy points that connect to and affect your entire body. By singing, speaking, or whispering mantras you are touching these energy points in a specific order and pattern that has a harmonious and healing effect on your physical, mental, and spiritual energy. The ancient science of mantras helps you reactivate nadis, concentrate, and still your mind.

The healing effect of the sound resonates with each chakra. For example, when singing OM, you are affecting your entire body beginning at the First Chakra and ending at the Seventh. For a clear demonstration of the harmonious effect of sound on your body, take a long, deep breath and slowly sing A-E-I-O-U-M. sound

Feel the sound as it travels from your lower spine and ends with MMM in your forehead. The healing vibration of this sound has affected your entire body. Combining mantra practice with Mudra practice magnifies these ancient self-healing techniques and lets you experience multidimensional healing.

HOW TO GET STARTED

The routines in this book are found in the sections on body, mind, and spirit. You may find yourself attracted to a specific Mudra, or to an area you wish to improve. Choose a routine that appeals to you strongly and practice each Mudra for three minutes.

Be still at least two minutes after you've completed the routine. There are many ways to tailor your practice.

- You may repeat the suggested affirmation with each Mudra. With each inhalation and exhalation repeat the affirmation once.

- If you choose to practice the mantra, repeat the mantra with each exhalation.

- You may visualize the healing colors connected to the Mudra surrounding your entire body or the corresponding chakra area.

- You may practice only the Mudra and just concentrate on you breath. Proper breathing is extremely important in whatever way you decide to practice.

- When you practice a three - Mudra routine, you may do each one differently. For example, a mantra with the first Mudra, an affirmation with the second, and visualization of color with the third. Enjoy making your practice personal and keep it fresh and interesting.

Keep in mind that we all are different and our experiences will vary daily. Certain days you may feel instant results and other days will be subtler. It is perfectly normal to feel overcome by laughter or tears during your practice, as you are releasing many pent-up, stressful, or toxic energies. Enjoy the experience and the profound peace, inner happiness, and power that the practice of Mudras will bring you.

Mudra for Sixth Chakra - Truth

Part One

Nature and You

I was born a child of nature. I would look at every tree very carefully. Is it easy to clim to? Will I break a branch and hurt the tree? I knew that if a tree branch breaks, the tree cries. I could actually feel the pain and tears of a tree. There was no greater joy for me than climbing to the very top of our apple tree and observing the birds for hours. I wanted to fly and be one of them.

My family and I would go to the forest on the weekends and walk for hours. The trees were much higher there and impossible to climb. The forest ground was soft; every step would sing with the sound of fallen leaves. At one end of the forest was a large hillside covered with wildflowers. We would roll down the flower-strewn hill and roar with laughter. Occasionally we would see a deer or a rabbit. We never wanted to leave the forest, and it would take us quite a while to get back into the car and drive home.

We also had a lot of animals. My mother was always rescuing baby birds that had fallen from their nests and for a while we lived with a special pet: a magpie. Many dogs and cats ruled our household, and I loved to collect snails and observe them for hours as they ate salad in slow motion. Then there was a time when we salvaged fifty frogs from a dry puddle. They lived in out tiny play pool until they were full-grown. Then they were transported into the wild. Watching them was like watching a different universe. I tell you this so you know what a lover of nature I am. Simply put, I adore nature and all living creatures.

Therefore writing about Mudras and nature has been a privilege and the fulfillment of a great desire.

RECONNECTING WITH YOUR GODDESS POWER

Imagine a glorious red rose. See the velvet petals open up to the sun. It's perfect. Take a few deep breaths and let its fragrance permeate your body. The essence of the rose is now with you.You are now the flower, every flower in nature.You have connected with Mother Nature.Learn to enjoy the moment. When you experience the inevitable dormant cycle, keep in mind you will blossom again. The Goddess of Nature is with you every step of the way. She nurtures you throughout your childhood and is with you when you breathe your last breath.

Do you remember your days as a little girl? How you enjoyed running outside? You adored your pet-or always wanted one- and could play for hours in the grass, sand - or mud! Would you like to feel that closeness to nature again? Would you like to laugh again from the depths of your soul? You can. Mother Nature hasn't changed; you have. You may have forgotten to listen to the birds, lie in the grass, and look up at the clouds.

When was the last time you really smelled a fragrant flower or sat at peace daydreaming and gazing into the distance? I will guide you back to that inspired feeling. I will take you on a journey that will remind you where you are from. You will find the happy childhood laughter that you lost and become a Goddess of Nature yourself. You will travel the sea, hug trees, and become a bird for a day, a week, a month, or a lifetime. You will feel the raindrops on your cheeks and hear the roar of the ocean. You will breathe again, and become a picture of tranquility. You will learn to experience Mudras, the ancient hand gestures that unlock the powers within, while you embrace and remember the healing powers of nature. You will remember your essence, reconnect with Mother Nature, and reagin that glow of the child who played in the yard all afternoon.

She is filled with nothing but laughter and joy. She is you. Reconnecting with Mother Nature will also remind you of your Goddess sisters. They are everywhere...running about, taking care of families, giving birth to babies, having trouble with husbands, and taking care of their parents. They are competing with you at work, they are looking at your man, and they may hurt you in order to save themselves.

The old tribal survival instincts and fears, the nervous glance at the clock ticking, and the never-ending mind games. The world today as we know it has forgotten about the feminine Goddess essence. We have forgotten who we are.

All women and your sister Goddesses. They go through similar experiences as you do, and they feel at times alone, as you do. Now you will remember who you are and remind them who they are. We are in this together; we're all connected, the Goddess of Creation and Nature. Connecting and embracing your sisters will be your gift to yourself. By reclaiming your power you will empower everyone around you and teach them how to listen to Mother Nature again. This is your journey to becoming a true goddess on earth. I hope that the pages will turn like the leaves of creation and I believe and pray that this journey will bring you much happiness, joy and health.

You are now familiar with all the important aspects of the Mudra practice. I would like to take you even deeper into the healing experience and reconnect you with nature while you practice Mudras.

HOW TO PRACTICE THESE CHAPTERS

The nature chapters are an additional tool for your self-healing and rejuvenating Mudra practice. The visualization journeys are short and easy to remember. You can read the chapter, close your eyes, and visualize the journey.

Practice the Mudra depicted with each chapter or choose any of your favorite Mudras to accompany the particular exercise. These chapters will expand your awareness of nature and remind you of your everlasting connection with every living essence of our world. With these visualizations, you will easily achieve inner peace, a tranquil mind, and self-healing. With the power of your mind, you can transport yourself in a matter of seconds to heaven on earth.

In your mind anything is possible. No matter where you are, if you imagine the glorious ocean and see the waves, your breath will slow down and your mind will expand. Transport yourself to a natural paradise. Drink the healing power of the environment and replenish your soul. What use is living in a flower garden when you never smell the flowers? Learn to enjoy the treasures of nature and the healing effects that they offer. Rekindle your sensitive, delicate feminine energy and invigorate your spirit.

Protect, cherish, and remain connected with your source of love and life. Be in tune, in charge, and then surrender.

1. Animal

Think about all different kinds of birds. Choose one that is your favorite.
Is it an eagle, a seagull, a dove, a swan, or maybe a peacock?

See the bird standing in front of you. It is beautiful, standing perfectly still and looking at you. Look into its eyes and connect with its soul. Imagine becoming the bird you see.
With ease, look around and observe the world through bird's eyes.

Take flight and lift yourself effortlessly high up toward the sky. You're flying above treetops and buildings, higher and higher. The human world seems farther away and smaller with each second. Now you are flying way above the city, underneath the clouds. You are free of worries and fears. You have no responsibilities or deadlines. All you do is fly wherever your heart desires. Fly above cities, meadows, mountaintops, and rivers.

When you need to, rest on a treetop and sing a beautiful song. Hear other birds answer you. You feel light and fast and love soaring in the sky. Fly as long as you wish

When you are ready, return to your home. Look at it from high up in the sky and see how small it is. See your human self sitting below.

You are ready to return. You are back, feeling content, light in your heart, and expanded in your mind. Now you know how small the problems are in the small world of yours.

Your vision has expanded. By changing your perspective you have changed your world. V

ast possibilities are available to you. All you need to do is lift yourself out of your world and look at everything from your bird's point of view.

Feel free and know all possibilities are open.

You are creating your life an every day has the potential for innumerable adventures.

You are free.

Mudra of Two Wings and Two Hearts

Sit with a straight spine and form a circle with each index finger and thumb, keeping your other fingers spread out. Lift your arms up in front of your heart, left over right, palms facing outward, and cross your hands at the wrists. Hook your pinkies together, keeping all fingers extended, and hold for at least three minutes.

BREATH
Long, deep, and slow.

2. Crystal

Find a crystal that resonates with you. A crystal that you feel a connection with. It can be small or large, any color.

After you make you choice, and have selected your crystal, carefully cleanse it in the sunlight, sea, or salt water for a few days. Hold it in your hand and feel its energy.

Within your crystal is a guiding life force or spirit. It makes the crystal grow and permeates it with healing powers.

You can hold your crystal, wear it, or place it near you.

Sit still and cross your hands over your chest, left hand first.

Breathe with the long, deep, and slow breath.

Close your eyes and visualize a soft violet light surrounding your crystal.

Now the light grows bigger and envelops you. The healing protective spirit of the crystal is directly connected to you.

Bathe yourself in the violet healing color of your crystal and thank it.

Whenever you encounter challenging situations, take your crystal and hold it in your hands. Close your eyes and concentrate on its powerful healing energy.

Your crystal is your protective friend, ready to share its energy with you anytime.

Mudra of Protection

Cross your left hand over right and place your palms on your upper chest.
Hold and feel the immediate energy shift.

BREATH
Long, deep, and slow.

3. Flowers

You are lying on a most comfortable flower bed. Close your eyes and relax. See a beautiful red rose. The petals are velvety and rich in color. Smell it and breathe with it.

Visualize this rose in your First Chakra. Concentrate and open all the petals. The rose is in full bloom, vibrant and glowing with beauty. Repeat our loud or in your mind:

CHAKRA 1. **" I am activating my center of vitality. It is healthy, powerful, and full of life energy."** Breathe and relax.

See a beautiful orange rose and place it in your Second Chakra. Feel its vibrancy and observe its beauty. All the petals are wide open.

CHAKRA 2. **"I am recharging my center of creativity and sexuality. It is healthy, powerful, and full of life energy."** Breathe and relax.

See a glorious yellow rose. Observe the tender petals and mesmerizing scent. Concentrate and see it clearly in your Third Chakra. Slowly inhale and exhale.

CHAKRA 3. **"I am recharging my emotional and mind center. It is healthy, powerful, and full of life energy."** Breathe and relax.

See a mesmerizing pink rose. It is fully open and uniquely scented. Place it in your heart area, the Fourth Chakra.

CHAKRA 4. **"I am recharging my heart center of love. It is healthy, powerful, and full of life energy."** Breathe and relax.

See a unique blue flower. The petals are tender and delicate. The bloom is fully open. Place it in the area of your throat, the Fifth Chakra.

CHAKRA 5. **"I am recharging my center of communication and truth. It is healthy, powerful, and full of life energy."** Breathe and relax.

See a magical purple flower. The bloom is fully open and the scent is permeating your senses. Place it in the area of your Third Eye, the Sixth Chakra.

CHAKRA 6. **"I am recharging my intuitive center. It is healthy, vibrant, and full of life energy."** Breathe and relax.

See a divine white flower. Its beauty is beyond any you have ever seen. The petals are pure, open, and glowing with light.

CHAKRA 7. **"I am reconnecting with the heavens. I am healthy, vibrant, ever-protected, and full of divine energy."**

Breathe and relax.

The essence of healing flowers is with you.

All your chakras are open, vibrant, and heathy.

Mudra for Opening Your Heart Chakra

Lift your hands up in front of your heart and create a cup, palms facing up, fingers apart. Hold for three minutes and keep fingers stretched like little antennas that are bringing healing energy int your heart.

BREATH
Long, deep, and slow.

4. Grass Meadow

You have a secret getaway in your world of nature. It is a lush grass meadow filled with wildflowers.

Be adventurous. Take off your shoes and feel the life force beneath your bare feet. The grass will tickle you, massage you, poke you and soothe you. The unusual feeling gets more comfortable with every step you take.

Suddenly you feel daring, out of the ordinary, and younger. You're instantly taken back to your childhood when you ran around barefoot, careless, without worries or fears. You are a child again and it doesn't matter if your feet get dirty; all that matters is having fun. Run around, hear your laughter and feel the excitement in your heart and soul. You are nature's child and it feels great. It is you, barefoot in the grass. Nature's magic carpet is underneath you. It grounds you and recharges you instantly.

Now sit down in the midst of the wildflowers and touch them with your hands. Let the fresh, natural scent permeate your senses. Look closely into the grass and notice the many blades that it takes to create the surface you're privileged to walk on. Brush the grass with your fingertips and feel the energy vibrate above the ground. The entire filed is alive! Each blade and wildflower is stretching toward the sunlight and drinking it up. The meadow grows warm in the sun and cools down at night; it waits through the winter and it revives in the spring.

The meadow is connected to every moment, every change; it stays vibrant, alive, and ever present. Inhale the vibrant energy and know that like every blade of grass and every wildflower you, too, will survive every change, adjust, grow, and drink the power from the sky above you. Your wildflowers will bloom again.

The soothing and nourishing energy of your meadow will always be in your heart in an instant. Just call for that picture with your mind.

Anytime, anyplace, take yourself back to your meadow and see yourself sitting, or running barefoot, and laughing with the joy of an adventurous child. Take it with you wherever you go. You are a child of nature.

Mudra for Creativity

Sit with a straight spine. Connect the thumb and index fingers, keeping the rest of the fingers straight. Bend your elbows and lift your hands to your sides, palms facing up at a sixty-degree angle to the body. Concentrate on your Third Eye and meditate for at least three minutes.

BREATH

Short, fast breath of fire from the navel.

5. Ocean

You are sitting at the edge of the most glorious and immense ocean. The sound of it roars in your ears and the waves are furiously rushing toward you. Each wave and sparkle is alive with immeasurable life forms.

You feel the salty air on your face and your lungs are filling up with vibrant and nurturing energy.
Close your eyes and give in to the sound of the ocean. This is the sound of the Universe.
The larger-than-life hum is the sound that can be heard anywhere if you fine-tune your ears to it.

It is the sound that permeates all living creatures.
The sound of the energy in all trees and flowers.
The sound of pulsating blood in your veins and those of every human being.
The sound of galaxies moving about.
The sound of life everlasting.

Connect to this sound. It instantly recharges and empowers you.

Open your eyes and look around you. You notice a beautiful conch lying next to you.

Pick it up and lift it to your ear. Like a magical music box it contains the exact replica of the ocean sound. It resonates with it and you can bring it as close to you as possible.

It is the sound of the Universe.
It is yours and available to you always and forever.
It will protect you, nurture you, and guide you.

You can carry the conch with you wherever you need it.

The magical sound of the power of the universe is right there for you to hear.
Listen and be one with the Universe.

Mudra for Listening Power

Hold your hands up at the left side of your face. Palms are not touching and are slightly cupped as if you are holding an imaginary conch. The left palm faces forward and the right palm is facing to your left. Concentrate on opening and magnifying your hearing with the left ear.

BREATH
Long, deep, and slow.

6. Lake

There is a glorious emerald green lake that awaits you. It is hidden in a sacred forest and visible only to your eyes. You always knew in your heart that this lake exists, but today is the day you will finally get to see it.

Close your eyes. Breathe and relax.
Suddenly you find yourself in front of a glorious sparkling green lake. There isn't a soul around, only you and the emerald green lake.

Step up to it and touch the water with your toes. It is very cold, crystal clear and clean.
Sit down at the edge of the lake and watch the calmness of the surface. Calm, steady, and vast.

This lake is your calm mind. There are no waves, there is no unrest. All is calm and steady. There is no one throwing pebbles into the lake. It is all you and your doing. If you want this lake to stay calm and steady, it will stay that way forever.

Sit at the edge of your lake and be still. Breathe and watch the surface. Feel a light breeze descend upon your face.

The lake responds with perfectly designed tiny sparkling ripples. Harmonious and beautiful, they let you know the lake is alive. Sensitive, and communicative.

Let a thought enter your mind and watch the lake answer. See how the water responds. The more harmonious the wave pattern, the more powerfully positive your mind is. Control the waves on your lake. Keep it calm, focused; let it dance in gentle, beautiful patterns. When you wish, calm it down to a standstill.

Play with different thought patterns and learn about the lake. It reflects you and every nuance that happens in your mind.

You may return to your lake whenever you wish. Let it respond to you and help you recognize positive and harmonious thought patterns.
You are creating it all.

Mudra for Calming Your Mind

Sit with a straight spine. Bend your arms in front of you and bring them up to chest level. Your elbows are bent at ninety-degree angle, your arms parallel to the ground. Place your right palm on top of your left arm and your left palm below your right arm, fingers together and straight. Hold for three minutes, making sure your arms don't sink, but stay at the same level. Relax and be still.

BREATH
Long, deep, and slow.

7. Rain

Look at the sky and notice the dark clouds gathering in a mysterious way. They look adventurous and powerful. The clouds are big and overwhelming, moving with an invisible and majestic force. Before you know it, here they are, right above you.

Suddenly you hear great thunder and small drops descend upon you with a slight hush. You are standing in the open without anything to protect you. You are going with the flow and embracing this experience, ready to be cleansed by nature.

Close your eyes and let the rain fall on your face, eyelids, cheeks, hair, hands, and body. Let it wash all your tension and troubles away and let them be soaked by the Earth. Taste the tears of the sky on your lips. The thirst in your heart is becoming satisfied. The beat of your restless heart is calming with the soothing sound of rain that grows louder and louder with each moment. The rain is cool and gentle. Let it fall on you. It is like a magic sprinkle of purifying tonic.

Listen to the soothing sound around you. Do you hear the leaves on the trees talking, the birds rejoicing, and the wind blowing the raindrops into specially designated directions? The drops are falling on your cheeks like the tears you forgot to shed. They are washing away any pain you carry with you and need to let go. The raindrops are pouring through your heart and cleansing every secret corner of unhappiness it hides.

Let it go, let it go, let it all be washed away, dissolved into the Earth. Breathe, fell the freshness in the air, and let your lips melt into a smile. Cry if you have to, cry with the rain. Cry with the clouds above you and feel them crying for you. The have the power to take the pain away. The sky may look dark, but the sun will shine again. Slowly the rain lets go and you sense just a few more drops falling. Delicately, like the strings on a harp, they dance their last dance and suddenly they're gone.

Breathe, and slowly open your eyes. Do you see the sparkling crystal clear sky above you? Do you hear the birds chirping and do you see the sunshine peeking through? The rays of sun find you and permeate your body with warm happiness.

Place your hands on your heart. Do you feel how light and free it is? All the pain and sorrow is gone; all that is left is pure happiness and love. Feel the glow from your heart magnify until it surrounds your entire being. You are reborn, recharged, and reconnected to your source. Take a breath, exhale, and smile.

Mudra for Universal Energy and Eternity

Sit with a straight spine and bend your elbows, holding your hands to your sides away from your body. Raise your palms to heart level, forming two V's. Palms are facing up and fingers are close together. Be still and feel the energy flowing into your hands. Relax and be still.

BREATH
Long, deep, and slow.

8. Tree

Find a tree. Go out into nature, or to a city ark, or just look through the window and find your tree. Is the tree big and roundly shaped, is it pointy and high, or maybe low to the ground with curvy strong branches?

Give your full attention to the tree. Notice it and make an effort to connect with it. Clearly observe the color of the leaves-are they light, dark? And the shape of the leaves-are they round, pointy? Notice the older leaves closer to the center and the new leaves toward the outer limits of the tree. The new leaves may have a different color; they are still growing. They are like little hands that are stretching toward the sky. If you can, touch the leaves gently and greet your tree. Feel the texture of the leaves. Now slowly touch the bark. Is it smooth and young or old, wise, and rugged? Feel its energy. Relax and notice the lovely smell of your tree. Is it a pine tree or maybe it is filled with blossoms? Let the magic healing smell permeate your sense. Feel the life current running through the trunk from the ground upward to the top of your tree. You are connected with this life force; its is permeating your hands and recharging your entire being. If you like, hug the tree. Hold it close to your heart and feel the life force within. Let your cheek touch the tree and let your skin feel the bark. Stand tall and proud with your tree. Be still, be quiet, listen, and just feel. Completely let go.

Open yourself up to another level of communication. Let the eternal power of your tree permeate every cell in your body. Receive love and give love in return. This love energy and vibration is what binds you and the tree. The tree is connected to Mother Earth in a profound way. Its roots are strongly holding Mother Earth and the bond is deep. The tree feels very secure with the ground. Now you feel very secure with the Earth. You are safe and connected, a part of it all. The tree has amazing healing power and energy. It shares it with you lovingly in an instant. It is full of magic; it reminds you of your magic.

A thought may suddenly enter your mind, maybe the answer to a question you have had. A loving, sweet word that you needed to hear. This tree is your friend. You can confide in it and it will always be there for you. Patiently and lovingly it will listen to your thoughts and inner conversations. It will help you remember the nature and sweetness of your soul, the patience that you were born with. Thank the tree, send it loving energy; it will feel it and return it tenfold. You have found a friend for life. From now on, look at all trees, pay attention to them, their sound in the wind. They will talk to you, soothe your senses, and heal your heart. Wherever you go they will wait for you, hear you, and talk back if you listen carefully. Let's protect all the trees of this world.

Mudra for Patience

Sit with a straight spine. Make circles with your thumbs and middle fingers, leaving the rest of your fingers outstretched. Lift your arms up at your sides so that your hands are at the level of your ears, the palms facing outward. Hold for three minutes, keeping your elbows nice and high. Relax and be still.

BREATH
Long, deep, and slow.

9. Sand

You are sitting on a golden sandy beach.

Feel the breeze of the ocean. The air is warm and moist with salt.

The ocean is roaring in the distance. You can feel the hot sand underneath you.

Stretch your hands and touch the sand. Feel the little grains slip through your fingers.

Inhale and fill your hand with sand. Exhale and let the sand slowly slip out of your hand.

Each time your hand is full of sand, inhale and soak in the golden light from it.

Each time you exhale, the sand slips away and the tension leaves your body and you get lighter.

Repeat fifteen times.

Now sit still and see yourself becoming smaller and smaller. You are as small as the sand grains bathing in the golden light. You are one with the golden light all around you.

A big hand lifts you with the sand grains off the ground and up.

Your body is completely light and completely connected to other sand grains. And now slowly...you slide to the ground.

You lose yourself in the motion of time.

You are one with the sand and one with the beach.

You are connected to each and every smallest particle of this Universe.

Mudra for Finding Perfect Truth

Sit with a straight spine. Place both hands on your knees, palms facing up toward the sky and very lightly cupped. Hold, concentrate on your Third Eye, and enjoy the stillness and peace.

BREATH
Long, deep, and slow.

10. Stone

A stone has a long history. It carries vibrations of the far past and stillness of the unknown future.

It seems that a stone doesn't move, but Mother Nature takes her stones on many journeys. They are her sacred children.

The world as we know it could not exist without stones. A stone may not seem as alive as you and I, but it has veins, bruises, sometimes fossils, and many memories from the past. You can learn stillness and strength from a stone.

Find a stone that you like. Maybe you can find one in the park or in the garden.

Hold it in your hand, observe its colors and feel the texture.

Its hard surface may have some ridges and if you soak it in water it will surprise you and completely change colors.

A stone is cold, but it warms up to you.

Suddenly you notice something unusual in your stone. A tiny ridge and a bump make it look almost like it has a nose...it could have a face. You see in it something no one else can. It's your magical stone with a secret face. Feel how resilient and strong it is. You have that kind of strength within you.

Now sit in stillness with your stone.

Place your hands and palms together in front of you. Press the fingertips together while spreading the fingers apart. Breathe long and deep.

Connect with your stone and feel its strength. Become one with your friend.

Recognize and embrace the Universal energy in every stone of this world.

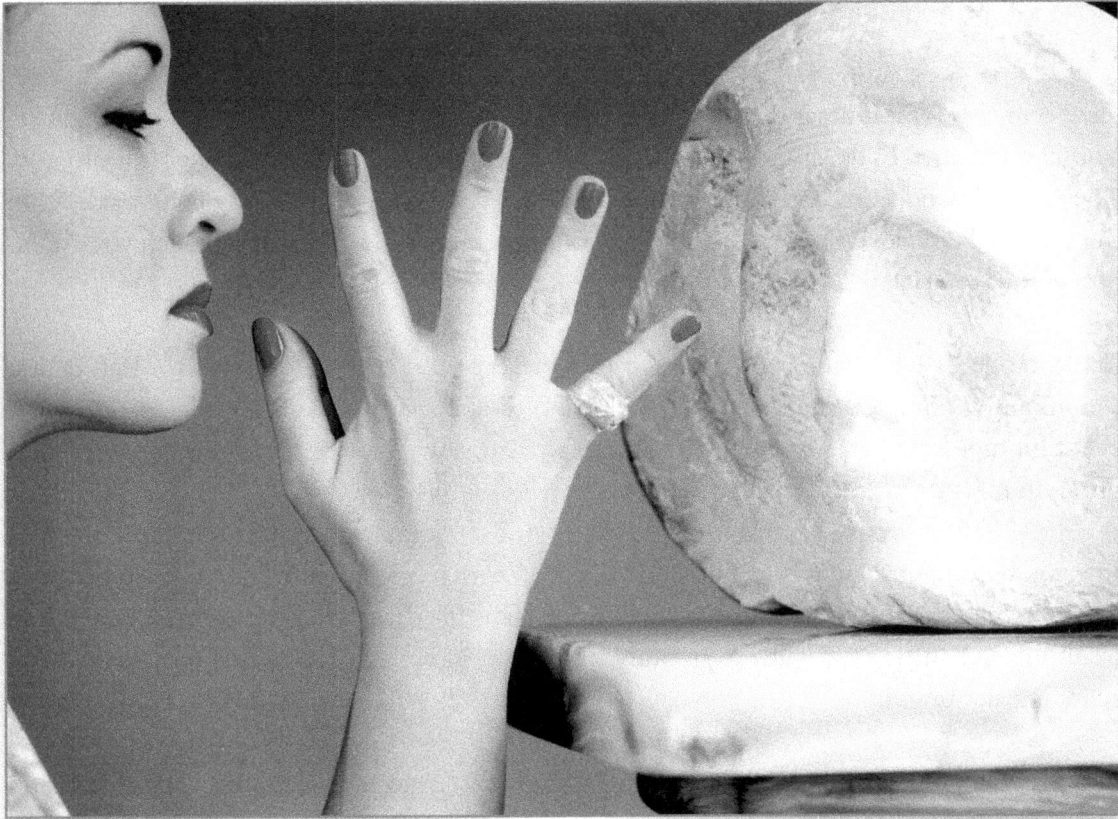

Mudra for Strength

Sit with a straight spine. Lift your hands up in front of you and touch your palms together, fingers spread apart. Apply maximum force to the ring and little fingers. Concentrate on the pressure of your fingers and hold for three minutes. Then relax, stretch your arms high above your head, let them down easy, and rest.

BREATH
Long, deep, and slow.

11. Snow

Have you ever looked up at the night sky while it is snowing?
You can try now. Look up and see the galaxy of snowflakes that are dancing toward you. They are light and fluffy, sparkling with freshness. They seem to have a tiny light inside them that makes them glow. They are landing on your cheeks and melting as they touch your skin. Stretch out your hand and catch a few.

Look at one closely. The intricate design and perfect geometry are astonishing. Before you can admire it completely, a snowflake melts and disappears. It was in your hand only for a beautiful moment. Catch another one and enjoy its beauty. Notice that it is very similar yet different in its formation. There are no two snowflakes alike.

Imagine becoming a snowflake. Surround yourself with a bright white light and see beautiful geometry all around you. It is the field of your aura, filled with healing light and energy in beautiful and intricate detail. Your body and your snowflake formation around you are sparkling and bright.

Imagine yourself floating weightless in the sky. Fearlessly go where the wind takes you and enjoy the moment. Notice other snowflake creations all around you. All are different, yet the same light shines from them all. You are all a part of the same light force that created you. You are never alone in the sky and the wind carries you where you need to go. Everyone has a predesignated journey.

Now you are coming closer to the ground. With ease you land and melt into the Earth.
Your form disappears, but your light remains. You have just changed appearance. When you're ready you can lift yourself up toward the sky and become a snowflake again, any time you wish.

Each time enjoy your slow descent toward the Earth and cherish each moment of the journey. The destination will be different each time and you will meet other snowflakes on the way. Your light is ever-present and you will always be protected and looked after on your windy flight. Only your form, perception, and experiences will be different.

Learn from each journey and let yourself be surprised, and guided.
They joy is in the flight.

Mudra for Heart Communication

Sit with a straight spine. Form circles with your thumb and index fingers and stretch out the rest of your fingers. Bending your elbows, lift your hands up to the level of your heart, and hold them with your palms facing out.

BREATH
Long, deep, and slow.

12. Waterfall

You are walking on a narrow forest path. In the distance you hear the mysterious and vibrant sound of a waterfall. You have never seen it before and know that you must find it. Follow the path. The sound is coming closer and closer. It seems that at any moment you will discover the source. Yet the path is winding and mysterious. You sense a coolness in the air. The sound is getting louder and louder. The path is winding around huge rocks.

Finally, beyond a particularly large rock, you discover the most glorious waterfall. Pure fresh water is pouring from an opening in the mountain and the water is gushing into a bubbly, foamy stream. There are many rocks in the stream and you find one that seems to be waiting just for you.

Sit down on the rock and listen to the sound of the waterfall above you. It is so near that you can feel misty sprinkles on your face. Your entire being is refreshed and purified just by sitting close to this majestic power. The waterfall is strong and steady, its source is Mother Earth. It has been here forever and seems very old yet ever fresh. Look at the waterfall. See how fast and strong the water streams down and falls fearlessly onto the rocks.

This waterfall is your unlimited creative power. Never-ending, strong, and steady. Pure, courageous, and powerful. Open yourself up to that ever-available creative energy that surrounds you. You are as close to the source as you wish. It is there for you night and day, strong and steady.

Absorb its power and let it fill your energy field. You are being recharged, you're in the flow, and in harmony with creation. You are an intrinsic and instrumental part of it. Take a deep breath and absorb this power that has been graciously given to you. You have been granted access to the sacred waterfall of creative power. Now you are replenished and nurtured.

Thank the waterfall for its gifts, breathe, and be still for a while. When you're ready, get up and find the path that you came from. You are strong, recharged, and ready to return to your life.

Whenever you need or want to, you can find your waterfall and replenish your creative energy. The waterfall is yours to visit and drink from. It is always there.
All you have to do is return to your secret path and find it.

Mudra of Divine Worship

Sit with a straight spine. Bring your palms together in front of your chest.
Concentrate on your Third Eye center.

BREATH
Long, deep, and slow.

Part Two

I Listen to My Body

Your body absorbs, responds, and reflects your emotional state at all times. It stored information from all the events of your life and responds accordingly.

It is important to listen to your body.

Every physical sensation is a message that needs to be heard and respected.

Don't ignore your body's voice...it will get unhappy and speak louder.
Lovingly tend to your body and it will miraculously carry you to magical places for many adventurous years to come.

1. The Teen Queen

The teenage years are filled with multidimensional changes. Feelings and perceptions about the world are changing daily. Emotions are overwhelming, uncontrollable; and the body is transforming overnight. It is essential for the parents of a teen to listen and to keep an open mind. Until now, you have been your child's most influential example of human interaction, relationships, and behavior.

When the inner search and life itself throws your teenager into the world, you must be the anchor of strength; you can help your child find her life's purpose. Your teenager knows more than you think. Be respectful and understanding; don't be over critical; and most of all teach your child how to respect and love others and herself.

Be aware of the powerful vibration a single negative sentence can leave in the mind of your sensitive and delicate teenager. Therefore as much as you may get irritated and aggravated by your teen's inconsiderable or bad behavior, the key is to respond with a calm, strong, and positive mind. You will see a big difference.

You can practice these Mudras with your child or alone. If your child is open to the practice, expand to other routines.

THE FIRST MUDRA will help you open and activate the communication channel with your teenager. Doing this practice together could be a perfect opportunity for creating closeness.

THE SECOND MUDRA will help the self-confidence and inner security of your child, which will help her resist negative people and actions.

THE THIRD MUDRA will help expand the upper level of the body for a better and confident posture and will help send energy into the upper chakras.

Mudra for Better Communication

AFFIRMATION
I AM OPEN TO LISTENING,
UNDERSTANDING,
AND SPEAKING

CHAKRA
BASE OF THE SPINE 1
REPRODUCTIVE ORGANS 2

HEALING COLOR
RED, ORANGE

MANTRA
RAA MAA
(I Am in Balance Between the Sun and the Moon, the Earth and the Ether)

Sit with a straight spine. Connect the index finger and the thumb, creating a circle. Stretch out the rest of the fingers and rest your hands, palms facing down, on your thighs. Hold for three minutes, breathe and relax.

BREATH
Long, deep, and slow.

Mudra for Inner Security

AFFIRMATION
I AM A UNIQUE, LOVELY HUMAN BEING;
I AM SECURE AND CONFIDENT WITH MYSELF

CHAKRA
SOLAR PLEXUS 3
HEART 4

HEALING COLOR
YELLOW, GREEN

MANTRA
AD SHAKTI AD SHAKTI
(I Bow to the Creator's Power)

Sit with a straight spine and place your hands in reversed prayer pose: hands touching back to back at the level of your heart and solar plexus. Hold the pose for a beat, then repeat with palms pressed together in a prayer pose, thumbs against the chest. Hold for a beat and repeat.

BREATH
Long, deep, and slow.

Mudra for Energy in Upper Chakras

AFFIRMATION
WITH EACH BREATH
I EXPAND MY ENERGY
AND MAGNIFY MY AWARENESS

CHAKRA
THROAT 5, THIRD EYE 6, CROWN 7

HEALING COLOR
BLUE, INDIGO, VIOLET

MANTRA
SAT NAM
(Truth Is God's Name, One in Spirit)

Sit with a straight back and place your hands above your head, palms pressed together, elbows to the side. Inhale and raise your hands as if someone were pulling them up. Exhale and lower your hands to a few inches above your head, palms always pressed together. Repeat for three minutes.

BREATH
Inhale slowly when lifting hands,
and exhale deeply when lowering hands.

2. PMS

PMS is not a one-week-a-month experience. It actually reflects your feelings, diet, exercise, mental state, and actions of the entire month. If you have had an emotionally stressful or physically difficult month, chances are that PMS will affect you on a deeper level.

It is essential to pay attention to your body ahead of time and develop a daily routine for a healthier and happier you. Negative emotions and the buildup of toxins are the main reason for PMS. Eliminating negative emotions should become your daily routine. Regular practice of the breath of fire-short, fast breathing-will help you maintain your reproductive health throughout the month. However, breath of fire is not recommended during your cycle.
Eat a healthy diet throughout the month and make sure you consume plenty of organic vegetables and fruits. Keep your diet as alkaline as possible and stay away from sugar, gluten, starch and junk food of any kind.

Daily practice of these Mudras will transform and reduce your monthly challenge and help you keep a balanced mental and emotional state during the cycle.

THE FIRST MUDRA will help you regain emotional balance when you feel upset, emotionally weak, and unstable.

THE SECOND MUDRA will help you regain mental stability when you feel out of control and your mind does not want to listen to you.

THE THIRD MUDRA will help balance and recharge your Second Chakra and your reproductive system.

Mudra for Emotional Balance

AFFIRMATION
I SURROUND MYSELF WITH LOVE;
I AM LOVED AND PROTECTED

CHAKRA
ALL

HEALING COLOR
ALL

MANTRA
SAT NAM

(Truth Is God's Name, One in Spirit)

Before this practice, drink a glass of water to balance the water in your system. Sit with a straight spine and place your hands with palms open under your armpits. Close your eyes, give yourself a hug, inhale and lift your shoulders toward your ears for a few moments; then exhale, lower your shoulders and relax. Repeat for three minutes.

BREATH
Long, deep and slow, observe your emotions calming down.

Mudra for Mental Balance

AFFIRMATION
MY MIND IS CALM, ALL IS WELL,
I AM AT PEACE AND
IN HARMONY WITH THE UNIVERSE

CHAKRA
ALL

HEALING COLOR
ALL

MANTRA
GOBINDAY, MUKUNDAY, UDARAAY,
APAARAY, HARYING, KARYNG, NIRNAMAY, AKAMAY
(Sustainer, Liberator, Enlightener, Infinite, Destroyer, Creator, Nameless, Desire-less)

Sit with a straight spine and place your hands at solar plexus level in front of you and interlace the fingers backward with palms facing up. Fingers are pointing up and the thumbs are straight.

BREATH
Long, deep, and slow.

Mudra for Your Reproductive Center

AFFIRMATION
MY CENTER OF CREATIVITY
IS REPLENISHED
WITH THE UNIVERSAL POWER

CHAKRA
REPRODUCTIVE ORGANS B2

HEALING COLOR
ORANGE

MANTRA
SAT NAM

(Truth Is God's Name, One in Spirit)

Sit with a straight spine. Place your left hand with palm facing down in front of your stomach area. Hold your right hand open, away from your body, the palm facing up.

BREATH
Long, deep and slow.

3. Instant Facial

Everyday stress is instantly reflected in your face. Before you know it, the pleasant expression is gone and you look worried and tired.

To keep a youthful appearance regardless of your age, you have to eliminate all negative mental energies that you may carry with you. You can have the most vigorous facial treatment at the beauty salon, but if your emotions are not at peace, the only difference you will notice will be in your wallet. Next time, prepare yourself with this routine before your facial pampering and really reap the benefits. Intense breathing will instantly bring needed oxygen to your cells and your entire face will glow as if you've just had it scrubbed and treated with a magic potion.

A healthy diet, avoiding gluten, excess amounts of sugar, fats and deep-fried foods, adds to proper care of your skin and face. Alcohol and smoking are your absolute enemies. In addition to a healthy lifestyle and positive disposition, the best secret for a glowing, youthful face is the breath of fire used in the second Mudra. Practice this one every day for a few weeks. You will notice immediate results already the first time, however with extended practice your face will be transformed. Later you may reduce the practice to a few times a week for lasting effects. This is an ongoing process. Make it apart of your regular routine and your entire being and your face will vibrate at a lighter and brighter level.

THE FIRST MUDRA will immediately help you recover and replenish your system from the damage of exhaustion.

THE SECOND MUDRA will help eliminate the traces of aging and help you straighten out those worry lines.

THE THIRD MUDRA will help evoke your inner beauty so it will be reflected on your glowing and rejuvenated face.

Mudra for Rejuvenation

AFFIRMATION
I AM RELEASING ALL STRESS;
I AM RELAXED AND CALM

CHAKRA
THROAT 5, THIRD EYE 6, CROWN -7

HEALING COLOR
BLUE, INDIGO, VIOLET

MANTRA
OM
(God in His Absolute State)

Sit with a straight back. Place both palms directly on your ears. Massage your ears in a circular motion away from your face – counter clockwise. Listen to the sound of "the ocean" you create with the palms of your hands and continue for at least three minutes.

BREATH
Long, deep and slow.

Mudra for Anti-Aging

AFFIRMATION
I AM BRINGING REJUVENATION
AND HAPPY ENERGY TO MY FACE

CHAKRA
BASE OF THE SPINE 1
REPRODUCTIVE ORGANS -2

HEALING COLOR
RED, ORANGE

MANTRA
EK ONG KAR SA TA NA MA
(One Creator of Infinity, Birth, Death, and Rebirth)

Sit with a straight back and make circles with your thumbs and index fingers. Stretch out the other fingers and place your hands on your knees, palms facing up.

BREATH
Short, fast breath of fire, focusing on the navel.

Mudra for Evoking Inner Beauty

AFFIRMATION
I AM A BEAUTIFUL FLOWER
READY TO BLOOM

CHAKRA
SOLAR PLEXUS 3
HEART 4

HEALING COLOR
YELLOW, GREEN

MANTRA
OM
(God in His Absolute State)

Sit with a straight spine and lift your hands in front of your solar plexus. Interlock the fingers and hold the palms flat and wide open as if displaying a beautiful flower placed in your hands. Absorb its beauty.

BREATH
Long, deep and slow.

4. The Feminine Spirit

Feeling your feminine spirit is as essential as food, air, and sunlight. Celebrate your femininity and the gift of being a woman every day. Make time for yourself, pamper your body, mind, and spirit, and be an example of female beauty. A daily stretch when you wake up will let your body know that you care and are paying attention.

Thank every little part of your body-your amazing body that is so self-contained and perfect: your feet for carrying you around all day, your legs for taking you anyplace you want, your hands that are involved in just about every action, your body for nourishing your being, your heart for unconditionally beating for you, your back for being the core of your physical body, your neck for giving you the capacity to expand your vision, your head for observing, hearing, speaking, and thinking. Celebrate it, cherish it, worship your femininity.

Give yourself a daily present of fifteen minutes and choose any of the Mudra routines from this book that may suit your temperament. Make that your time alone so you can replenish, rejuvenate, and recharge yourself. Remember, you are a sensitive, delicate, and yet powerful woman, put on this Earth to teach others about all aspects of beauty, compassion, and unconditional love. Live it, feel it, and be it.

THE FIRST MUDRA will help you find and feel the strength that resides within you.

THE SECOND MUDRA will help you evoke your power of love and beauty.

THE THIRD MUDRA is an ancient Buddhist Mudra to help evoke the sacred heavenly scents while meditating. Pay attention to the different scents that may enter your mind and senses. Surprise yourself with this meditation for sensuality.

Mudra for Strength

AFFIRMATION
I AM A WOMAN, STRONG IN HEART AND MIND,
AND DELICATE IN GESTURES

CHAKRA
SOLAR PLEXUS 3
HEART 4

HEALING COLOR
YELLOW, GREEN

MANTRA
SAT NAM
(Truth Is God's Name, One in Spirit)

Sit with a straight back. Lift your hands up to the level of the heart and place your palms together. Fingers are spread apart. The thumbs are almost touching and the index and middle fingers are barely touching. Apply maximum force to the ring and little fingers. Concentrate on various pressures of our fingers, after three minutes relax, stretch arms above head, then let down easy and rest.

BREATH
Very long, deep and slow.

Mudra for Powerful Energy

AFFIRMATION
I AM ALL THINGS BEAUTIFUL; I REFLECT LOVE,
HAPPINESS, AND THE HARMONY OF NATURE

CHAKRA
HEART 4, THROAT 5, THIRD EYE -6

HEALING COLOR
GREEN, BLUE, INDIGO

MANTRA
OOOOONG
(God as a Creator in Manifestation)

Sit with a straight spine. Lift your hands in front of you at the solar plexus. Place your ring fingers flat and straight together and interlace all other fingers, the right thumb on top of the left.

BREATH
Long, deep and slow.

Mudra for Evoking
the Sacred Scent of Perfume

AFFIRMATION
I SEE A FLOWER AND ITS PETALS OPENING TO ME;
I SMELL THE DIVINE SCENT
OF THIS UNIQUE BLOOM

CHAKRA
HEART 4
THROAT 5

HEALING COLOR
GREEN, BLUE

MANTRA
OM
(God in His Absolute State)

Sit with a straight spine and lift your right hand to the level between your heart and throat, the palm facing toward the left hand. Lift the left hand and make a fist. With the flat lower part of your fingers, press your fist against the palm of your right hand. Apply gentle pressure and hold. Higher states of meditation while practicing this Mudra, will evoke a special magnified sense of sacred scent.

BREATH
Long, deep and slow.

5. Sexual Empowerment and Fertility

Human sexuality is an ever-present and fascinating topic. What attracts us to each other-our entire sexual behavior-often lacks logical explanation. Just when you think you've solved the mystery and have control over it, you are taken by surprise. Suddenly you're powerless and no rules apply. In order to experience the ultimate sexual pleasure you must expand your sexual self and connect it with your spirit.

The creative source that brought your spirit into this world was intertwined in a sexual dance. To understand and own your sexual power you must understand yourself. Control your power. Give it only when you want and to whom you want. Pay attention to your inner voice. Love, respect, self-confidence, and communication are key elements for a happy and fulfilling sexual relationship. To expand your sexual relationship, try engaging in a spiritual practice such as the second Mudra together with your partner. Even a few moments of stillness together will uplift and harmonize your joined vibration.

When you desire to create a new life, you need a healthy body, a calm, peaceful mind, and an open spirit. Fears, expectations, pressure, and insecurity can be in your way of getting pregnant. Self-empowering, healing, and relaxation practices are an essential part for your preparation. Nurture and balance your body, mind and spirit, listen to your inner voice, and communicate lovingly with your partner. Prepare yourself on a physical, mental, and spiritual level.

THE FIRST MUDRA will help you activate, balance, and control your sexual power.
THE SECOND MUDRA will help you balance the male and female aspects of your sexuality.
THE THIRD MUDRA will help you empower the reproductive center with healthy, vibrant energy that will help attract a new, harmonious spirit.

Mudra for
Activating the Lower Chakras

AFFIRMATION
I AM THE MASTER OF MY POWER

CHAKRA
BASE OF THE SPINE 1
REPRODUCTIVE ORGANS 2

HEALING COLOR
RED, ORANGE

MANTRA
SAT NAM
(Truth Is God's Name, One in Spirit)

Sit with a straight back. Place both hands at waist level, thumbs open with palms facing down. All fingers are stretched and together, the tips of the middle fingers an inch apart. As you inhale, concentrate on expanding the lower area of your stomach. When you exhale, contract the stomach and bring your fingertips closer until they almost touch. Concentrate on bringing vital creative life force energy into that area.

BREATH

Start slowly and after a minute increase your breathing into the breath of fire. After a minute, slow down and return to the slow, deep breath.

Mudra for Sexual Balance

AFFIRMATION
I LOVE, RESPECT, AND CHERISH MY BODY.
I CHOOSE A PATNER WHO LOVES, RESPECTS,
AND CHERISHES ME AS I CHERISH THEM IN RETURN

CHAKRA
REPRODUCTIVE ORGANS 2

HEALING COLOR
ORANGE

Sit with a straight back. With your elbows slightly to the sides, clasp your hands together. The fingers are intertwined. The right thumb on top of the left will empower the male side of your nature and the left thumb on top empowers the feminine, emotional side of your nature.

BREATH

Long, deep and strong.

Mudra for Lower Spine

AFFIRMATION
MOTHER EARTH IS RECHARGING MY BODY.
I AM THE MOTHER EARTH

CHAKRA
BASE OF THE SPINE 1
REPRODUCTIVE ORGANS 2

HEALING COLOR
RED, ORANGE

MANTRA
OM
(God in His Absolute State)

Sit with a straight back and make fists with both hands. Leave the thumbs stretched out and place hands on your knees. The palms are facing the ground and the thumbs are directed towards each other. Keep the fists strong and feel the energy pulsating in your palms.

BREATH
Long, deep and strong.

6. Weight Issues

Some of us are lucky and never have to face this problem, but most of us experience it sooner or later: that unattractive orange-peel skin that seems to appear out of nowhere and sends us running for towels all summer so the whole world doesn't see us in our bathing suits. But here's a fact that is true: you can get rid of cellulite. It's not the easiest thing to do and you have to be quite disciplined, but it can be done.

First and foremost, you must pay attention to your diet. Stay away from sugar, gluten, and carbohydrates. Do not eat past six PM and eat an alkaline organic diet, mostly vegetables and protein. Vigorously massage the affected area in the shower every morning or evening. Drink a lot of water with lemon so you cleanse your system. And last but not least, every day go for a walk, a bicycle ride, or practice yoga. Those are the keys to reclaiming your lovely thighs.

It is essential that while you're on the diet you maintain a proper mental attitude. Positive affirmations will help you stay strong in your mind about sticking to your discipline. Mudra practice will help you calm your mind, release toxins from your body, and heal your spirit. Often our weight is connected to our emotional state. When we hold on to emotional burdens and fears, our bodies will mentally hold on to the physical weight as well. Releasing the useless emotional baggage will result in loosing your excess physical weight. This routine will help keep you on track with any healthy diet plan that you choose to follow.

THE FIRST MUDRA will help you let go of excess negative energy that you may be holding on to that prevents you from letting go of the physical weight.
THE SECOND MUDRA will help you feel less hungry and will fill you with vibrant energy.

Mudra for Vitality and Letting Go

AFFIRMATION
I AM RELEASING ALL NEGATIVE ENERGY
AND AM MAKING SPACE FOR
THE NEW LIGHTER AND HEALTHIER ME

CHAKRA
BASE OF THE SPINE 1
REPRODUCTIVE ORGANS 2

HEALING COLOR
RED, ORANGE

MANTRA
SAT NAM
(Truth Is God's Name, One in Spirit)

Sit with a straight back and place your fists on your knees, palms facing up. Concentrate on your base chakra. Sit tall and attempt to stretch as if trying to get taller. Be aware of the ground underneath you and the life force of the Earth.

BREATH
Long, deep and slow.

Mudra for Help with a Diet

AFFIRMATION
I AM FOLLOWING MY HEALTHY DIET PLAN.
I AM LESS HUNGRY AND HAVE MORE

CHAKRA
BASE OF SPINE 1
SOLAR PLEXUS 3
CROWN 7

HEALING COLOR
RED, YELLOW, VIOLET

Sit with a straight back and extend your arms in front of you parallel to the ground, palms facing up, slightly cupped. Inhale and move your hands to the sides, as you exhale, return your hands to their original position in front of you, but with your palms facing each other. Keep the palms apart and be aware of the life force that is being magnified between your hands. Repeat.

BREATH
Long, deep inhalation as you expand the arms,
and exhalation as you return them in front of you.

7. Motherhood

Motherhood is undoubtedly one of life's most difficult and privileged assignments. From the moment you become a mother your life changes forever. Suddenly every decision is connected to your child.

You experience tremendous and indescribable joy while unfortunately you seem to lose any time for yourself.

To be the wonderful mother that you've always wanted to be, you must create a regular rejuvenation routine that you can follow, no matter what. If you cannot spare nine minutes as this routine requires, divide it into thee-minute practices.

Start your morning with the **FIRST MUDRA** for recharging. Get ready for your day by feeling fresh and full of energy.

THE SECOND MUDRA will immediately increase your energy when you feel worn out at any time during the day.

THE THIRD MUDRA will help you relax and enjoy your role as a mother. In the midst of all the responsibilities, it is important to experience the joy and happiness your child is giving you.

You can be, will be and are the greatest mother.

Mudra for Recharging

AFFIRMATION
MY ENTIRE BODY IS RECHARGED
WITH UNLIMITED POWER

CHAKRA
BASE OF THE SPINE 1
REPRODUCTIVE ORGANS 2
CROWN 7

HEALING COLOR
RED, ORANGE, VIOLET

Sit with a straight spine. Extend your arms in front of you, parallel to the ground, keeping your elbows straight. Make a fist with your right hand and wrap the left hand around the right fist. The bases of the palms are touching and the thumbs are straight up.

BREATH
Long, deep and strong.

Mudra for Preventing Exhaustion

AFFIRMATION
I AM RELAXING MY ENTIRE BODY

CHAKRA
SOLAR PLEXUS 3
HEART 4

HEALING COLOR
YELLOW, GREEN

MANTRA
SAT NAM
(Truth Is God's Name, One in Spirit)

Sit with a straight back. Lift your arms and grasp your earlobes with your thumbs and index fingers. Hold on to your ears and let the weight of your hands pull on them. Relax and feel the energy shifting in your head and body. Hold for three minutes and relax.

BREATH
Long, deep and slow.

Mudra for Relaxation and Joy

AFFIRMATION
I FEEL THE HAPPINESS AND JOY OF MOTHERHOOD;
I AM GRATEFUL FOR THIS GIFT

CHAKRA
SOLAR PLEXUS 3
HEART 4

HEALING COLOR
YELLOW, GREEN

MANTRA
HAREE HAR HAREE HAR
(God in His Creative Aspect)

Sit with a straight back and lift your hands up in front of your chest. Make a fist with your left hand, tucking the thumb inside. Wrap your right hand around the left and place your right thumb over the base of the left thumb. Concentrate on your Third eye area and hold for three minutes.

BREATH
Long, deep and slow.

8. The Ageless Goddess of Wisdom

You have lived a full life and learned invaluable lessons. Now it is time you teach the world to love, forgive, cherish, and dream just as you did in the past and still do today.

Your words of wisdom must be heard; your experiences can help others and your smile can tell a million truths. Share your experiences by teaching, talking, or writing your much valued lessons. Even if you have only one pupil, you can change her life.

Celebrate your wisdom and enjoy your timelessness. Share your insight and treasure your hard-earned wisdom.

Teach the world to respect and listen to you and learn to enjoy your golden years. The hard work is accomplished; now you can return to yourself and listen to your inner voice. There may be a dream still in need of fulfilling. This may turn out to be your most productive time yet.

THE FIRST MUDRA will help you let good memories permeate your heart and fill it with renewed optimistic and adventurous energy.

THE SECOND MUDRA will help you open your crown center and empower your direct connection with the source of universal wisdom.

THE THIRD MUDRA will help you protect your health so that you may enjoy your golden adventures.

Mudra for Uplifting Your Heart

AFFIRMATION
MY HEART IS FILLED WITH LOVE,
HAPPINESS, AND OPTIMISM

CHAKRA
HEART 4

HEALING COLOR
GREEN

Sit with a straight back and lift your arms up to shoulder level, elbows bent and parallel to the ground. Tuck your thumbs under your armpits and keep the rest of your fingers straight and together. Your hands should be above your breasts, palms facing down. As you inhale, the distance between middle fingertips gets bigger; as you exhale, the middle fingertips should touch or cross over each other. With each inhalation feel the healing energy expand your heart and chest area.

BREATH
Long, deep and slow.

Mudra for Opening Your Crown

AFFIRMATION
I AM CONNECTED TO AND PART OF

CHAKRA
CROWN 7

HEALING COLOR
VIOLET

Sit with a straight back and interlock your fingers, but keep the thumbs extended upward. Now bring your hands above your head so that your thumbs are pointed to the back. Hold for a minute and a half and feel the energy pulse in your thumbs as you keep them extended. Then lower your hands and bring them in front of your heart for minute and a half.

BREATH
Long, deep and slow.

Mudra for Protecting Your Health

AFFIRMATION
I AM HEALTHY, VIBRANT,
AND WILL BE SO
TOMORROW AND ALWAYS

CHAKRA
ALL

HEALING COLOR
ALL

MANTRA
OM
(God in His Absolute State)

Sit with a straight back. Bend your right elbow and lift your hand up, palm facing out. The index and middle fingers are pointing up; the rest are curled with the thumb over. Hold your left hand in the same Mudra with the two stretched fingers touching your heart. Hold for three minutes.

BREATH
Inhale for ten counts, hold the breath for ten counts,
and exhale for ten counts.

9. Protecting Your Electromagnetic Field

Many of us spend countless hours working at the computer or using the cellphone. It is important to take a break and recharge your system so that your auric field doesn't get drained by these powerful devices.

Make it a habit to get up and take a short walk away from the computer every couple of hours. Leave the cellphone behind and be free for a while. The world will still turn around the same way even without your constant following every move online or texting non essential conversations.

Stretch your body and take deep, long, and slow breaths. Working on the computer, writing, and reading are tremendous strains on your eyes. Therefore, take time out to give the proper exercise. Every two hours, take a three-minute break and practice the Mudra for healthy eyes. The entire routine can be practiced at any time, especially at the beginning and end of your workday. Make sure to turn your body away from the computer when practicing those Mudras.

THE FIRST MUDRA will keep your eyes healthy and strong. It is essential for everyone who wants to maintain great eyesight.

THE SECOND MUDRA will help you prevent exhaustion and burnout from long working hours.

THE THIRD MUDRA will activate and regenerate the area of your middle spine so that you can keep a straight posture and maintain strong energy in your solar plexus.

Mudra for Healthy Eyes

AFFIRMATION
MY EYES ARE HEALTHY AND RESTED

CHAKRA
THIRD EYE 6

HEALING COLOR
INDIGO

MANTRA
OM
(God in his Absolute State)

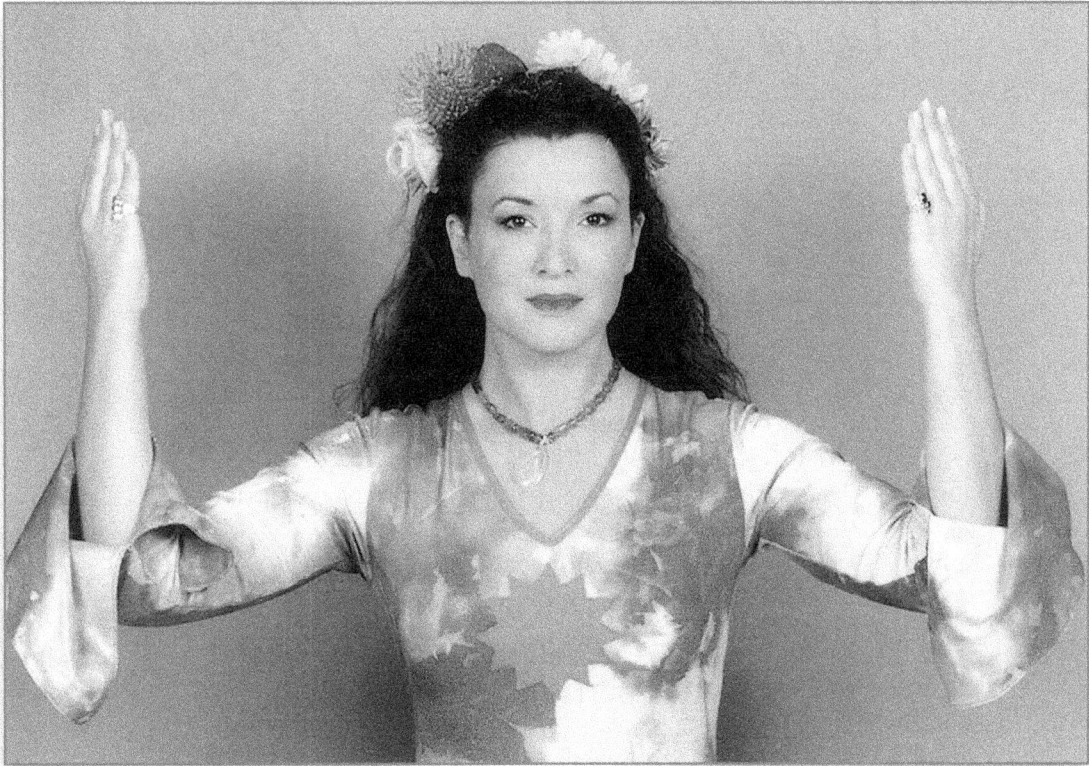

Sit with a straight spine. Bring your arms up, at your sides, the palms turned in toward you. Now bring your palms together in front of your face, as if drawing a curtain. Open your arms, inhale, and look into the distance. Exhale when bringing your hands in front of your eyes and readjust the focus and look into your palms. This Mudra should be practiced every two hours for three minutes when working at a computer.

BREATH
Long, deep and slow.

Mudra for Preventing Burnout

AFFIRMATION
I AM FILLED WITH HEALING ENERGY;
I AM RESTED AND REJUVENATED

CHAKRA
BASE OF THE SPINE 1
REPRODUCTIVE ORGANS 2
SOLAR PLEXUS 3

HEALING COLOR
RED, ORANGE, YELLOW

MANTRA
OM
(God in His Absolute State)

Sit with a straight spine. Bring your forearms up in front of you at heart level and bend your elbows to the side. With the palms facing the ground, fold your thumbs across the palm of each hand till they reach the bases of your ring fingers. Now bend your fingers slightly and touch the backs of your fingertips together, forming a V-shape with your hands. Hold for three minutes. Making sure your elbows remain elevated. Relax and rest.

BREATH
Long, deep and strong.

Mudra for Middle Spine

AFFIRMATION
I AM SENDING HEALING POWER TO MY BACK;
I CAN SIT STRAIGHT
AND FEEL STRONG AND RESTED

CHAKRA
SOLAR PLEXUS 3
HEART 4

HEALING COLOR
YELLOW, GREEN

MANTRA
OM
(God in his Absolute State)

Sit with a straight back and place your fists on your knees. Leave the thumbs pointing up. Concentrate on your thumbs, sending healing energy to the middle area of your back. Keep the thumbs stretched and hold for three minutes.

BREATH
Long, deep and strong.

Part Three

Be Still My Mind

The games that your mind plays with you usually prevent you from enjoying the present.

Here are some routines to conquer those scenarios that play over and over again in your mind and seem to have a hold on it. You can reprogram your mind and transcend those seemingly never-ending thoughts.

It is important that you have a desire to change...you're halfway there.

Find your most challenging obstacle that prevents you from being your best and practice the routine.

It is said that it takes forty days to change a habit, it takes ninety days to be firm in a new habit, and in one hundred twenty days the new habit becomes a part of your nature. Reprogram your mind the way you select and want to.

1. Time Is Your Friend

Time is ticking for all of us. Would you feel better if time didn't exist? In essence we are all timeless and everything is happening at precisely the perfect time. Even when we feel the timing is bad, there is a higher reason for it all. With time we grow, learn, and hopefully find inner happiness. Life passes quickly and we need to learn how to enjoy each and every moment of it. Otherwise we end up worrying and making plans about something that is already happening. To be here in the now, that is our purpose.

This moment-you reading this book-is your time. Take a breath and feel connected to all life at precisely this moment. Know there are millions and millions of people all around the world and we all breathe, live, love, and think abut time. At least once a month give yourself the present of timelessness. Forget all the clocks, take off your watch, turn off the phone and just be. No pressure, no rushing-just follow the daily rhythm with the Sun. Be aware of a different time, of sunrise and sunset. Listen to the birds. Observe the trees and their timelessness. Melt away the pressure of schedule.

You are an individual different from others, as is your timing. Never compare yourself to others. You will fulfill your desires at a time perfect for you and there are always higher reasons for it. Remember the old saying: time heals everything. The passing of time gives us the great gift of being able to distance ourselves from a particular situation and see the larger picture. You will discover that time is your teacher and your friend.

THE FIRST MUDRA will help you calm your mind so that you can release the tension, and open your awareness and understanding.

THE SECOND MUDRA will help you access the intuitive knowledge about perfect timing.

THE THIRD MUDRA will help you balance and understand the Yin and Yang in your life and recognize a destined and positive timing in everything.

Mudra for Calming Your Mind

AFFIRMATION
I FEEL CALM AND PEACEFUL

CHAKRA
SOLAR PLEXUS 3
CROWN 7

HEALING COLOR
YELLOW, VIOLET

MANTRA
OM
(God in his Absolute State)

Sit with a straight spine. Cross your arms in front of your chest, elbows bent at a ninety-degree angle and arms parallel to the ground. The right hand is on top of the left arm and left hand below the right arm. All fingers are together and straight. Hold and keep the arms from sinking for three minutes, then relax and be still.

BREATH
Long, deep and slow.

Mudra for Activating the Third Eye

AFFIRMATION
I AM AWARE OF PERFECT TIMING IN MY LIFE

CHAKRA
THIRD EYE 6

HEALING COLOR
INDIGO

MANTRA
OM
(God in his Absolute State)

Sit with a straight spine. Connect the thumb and index fingers and extend the rest of the fingers. Place your hands on your knees, palms facing up. Concentrate on your Third Eye and sit in complete stillness.

BREATH
Long, deep and slow.

Mudra for Balancing the Yin and Yang

AFFIRMATION
MY LIFE WORKS IN HARMONY, PERFECT BALANCE
AND TIMING OF THE UNIVERSE

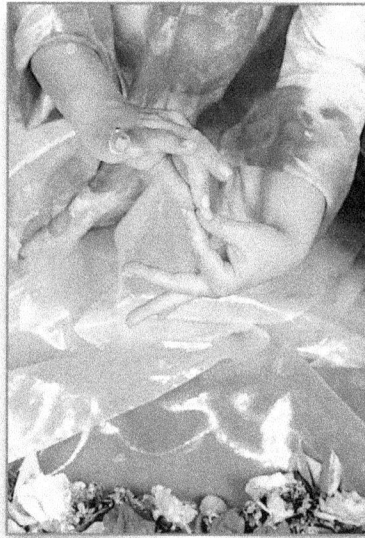

CHAKRA
ALL

HEALING COLORS
ALL

MANTRA
OM
(God in his Absolute State)

Sit with a straight spine. Connect the thumbs and index fingers, extending the rest of the fingers and spacing them apart. Lift your right hand up in front of your chest with the palm turned outward, the fingertips pointing left. Hold the left hand below the right in front of your stomach area, palm turned inward and fingertips pointing right. Now connect the thumbs and index fingers of both hands, creating the Wheel of Life.

BREATH
Long, deep and slow.

2. Embrace Change

Your life began with a big change. Your birth was most likely a profound change in your parent's lives. Every day while you were growing up, changes were present.

Life *is* all about change, yet we hesitate to change our daily routines, personal or business relationships, or careers. The fear of change is connected with the fear of loss.

Remember, many changes are for the better and very necessary. When you fell in love for the first time the profound change affected your entire being. There are also times when we wish a change would happen. But change is inevitable.

You may feel impatient and want to rush a change. It is important to be in tune with the divine energies and the perfect time for a change. You will observe in the end that everything will make sense. It is never too late for a change since your entire life can change with one phone call, in one moment, in one day.

Welcome change in your life, now and in the future, for it will bring you joy, love, happiness, new friends, and many adventures.

THE FIRST MUDRA will help you release the fears that are preventing changes from occurring in your life.

THE SECOND MUDRA will help you accept and welcome the changes that are occurring.

THE THIRD MUDRA will help you become patient when you want a change and can't seem to be able to wait another day.

Mudra for Facing Fear

AFFIRMATION
I AM FEARLESS

CHAKRA
SOLAR PLEXUS 3
CROWN 7

HEALING COLOR
YELLOW, VIOLET

MANTRA
NIRBHAO NIRVAIR AKAAL MORT
(Fearless, Without Enemy, Immortal Personified God)

Sit with a straight spine. Bend your right elbow and lift the arm up to the level of your face. Face your palm outward, as if taking a vow. Bring your left arm in front of your navel, palm facing up. Concentrate on energy being received into your palms and hold for at least three minutes.

BREATH
Long, deep and slow.

Mudra for Meditation of Change

AFFIRMATION
ALL GOOD THINGS COME WITH CHANGE
I ACCEPT AND WELCOME CHANGE INTO MY LIFE

CHAKRA
THIRD EYE 6
CROWN 7

HEALING COLOR
INDIGO, VIOLET

MANTRA
ONG NAMO GURU DEV NAMO
(I Bow to the Infinity of the Creator,
I call on the Infinite Creative Consciousness and Divine Wisdom)

Sit with a straight spine. Fold your fingers into fists, the fingertips pressing the upper pads of the hands. Press the backs of your hands together at the knuckles. The thumbs are extended and touching at the fingertips. Hold your hands in front of your navel with the thumbs directed slightly upward toward your heart.

BREATH
Long, deep and slow.

Mudra for Patience

AFFIRMATION
I KNOW ALL CHANGES
THAT I DESIRE AND WISH FOR
WILL COME TO ME AT A PERFECT TIME

CHAKRA
THIRD EYE 6
CROWN 7

HEALING COLOR
INDIGO, VIOLET

MANTRA
EK ONG KAR SAT GURU PRASAAD
(One Creator, Illuminated by God's Grace)

Sit with a straight spine. Connect the fingertips of the thumbs and middle fingers, creating a circle. The rest of the fingers are outstretched. Lift your arms up at your sides so that your hands are at the level of your ears, palms facing outward. Keep your elbows nice and high for three minutes.

BREATH
Long, deep and slow.

3. Understand Love

Understanding love is just as difficult as understanding that sometimes love makes no sense. The mind finds no logic, practicality, or convenience in love and will try to talk you out of it and remind you of past hurts and fears.

The mind will have a perfectly logical reason why you should not fall in love, why you should not follow your heart, and will encourage you to play games in matters of the heart. The heart, on the other hand, will throw you into the whirlwind and all else will disappear.

All you will see is the person you are in love with in the most glorious rainbow colors, the best and the brightest of everything. After the initial plunge you will start noticing that the colors have different shades and that there is more than just sunshine, there are also shadows. Now the mind will have a chance to speak out loud and remind you of your fears. We may all experience slightly different versions of it, this dance between the mind and the heart, but no matter what, we need to learn how to recognize the one and the other, balance them out, and achieve that wonderful state of harmony we all long for. It is possible, because it is *your* mind and *your* heart.

All you need to do is remind your mind that rules are meant to be broken and remind your heart to stay open, forgiving, and filled with endless love. You will be loved in return.

THE FIRST MUDRA will help you calm your mind when it tries to rationalize and justify matters of the heart.

THE SECOND MUDRA will help you open yourself to receive love and feel the flow of that power endlessly rejuvenating your soul.

THE THIRD MUDRA will help you connect with your loved one, accept your differences, and experience the true power of two hearts united in love.

Mudra for Tranquilizing Your Mind

AFFIRMATION
MY MIND IS CALM, QUIET, AND FILLED WITH PEACE

CHAKRA
SOLAR PLEXUS 3
HEART 4
THROAT 5
THIRD EYE 6

HEALING COLOR
YELLOW, GREEN, BLUE, INDIGO

MANTRA
MAN HAR TAN HAR GURU HAR
(Mind with God, Soul with God, the Divine Guide and His Supreme Wisdom)

Sit with a straight spine. Bend your elbows and bring your hands up to your chest. Connect the middle fingertips and stretch them outward. Bend the rest of the fingers and press them together along the second joint. Connect your thumb tips and extend them toward you.

BREATH
Long, deep and slow.

Mudra for Opening Your Heart Center

AFFIRMATION
I OPEN MY HEART AND MIND,
AND I LET LOVE BLEND THE TWO IN GOLDEN LIGHT

CHAKRA
HEART 4

HEALING COLOR
GREEN

MANTRA
SAT NAM
(Truth Is God's Name, One in Spirit)

Sit with a straight spine. Lift your hands up in front of your heart and create a cup, palms facing each other, all fingers spread and pointing up. The upper parts of your thumbs and pinkies and the bases of your palms are touching. Visualize opening your heart, keeping fingers outstretched.

BREATH
Long, deep and slow.

Mudra for
Two Hearts and Two Wings

AFFIRMATION
I ENJOY EVERY PRECIOUS MOMENT
OF PURE LOVE WITH MY BELOVED

CHAKRA
HEART 4

HEALING COLOR
GREEN

MANTRA
SAT NAM
(Truth Is God's Name, One in Spirit)

Sit with a straight spine. Connect the thumbs and index fingers, forming a circle. Extend all other fingers, keeping them spread out. Lift your arms up in front of your heart, left over right, palms facing outward, and cross your wrists over each other. Hook your pinkies together, keep all fingers extended, hold for three minutes.

BREATH
Long, deep and slow.

4. Release Hurt

We all carry within us painful memories and old wounds. Holding on to bad experiences prevents us from being open to new and happy events.

It may also be a comfortable habit to hang on to pain that you are familiar with. Maybe you are fearful of new hurtful experiences.

It is important to be honest with yourself and find your true feelings. With some soul-searching you can confront old pain and let it go.

Write on a piece of paper the painful memories that you carry within your heart. Write everything down that comes to mind. When you're done, let go of the paper. Throw it away or create a ritual and burn it.

When you consciously decide that you're ready to let go of the old and replace it with new happy experiences, you've come a long way.

Make a point of practicing this routine of Mudras every morning.
Prepare yourself for a new day of adventures and be open for happy events to come into your life.

THE FIRST MUDRA will help you heal old wounds.
THE SECOND MUDRA will help you open your heart and release the old and prepare for the new.
THE THIRD MUDRA will help you voice your difficult past experiences and release them.

Mudra for Self-Healing

AFFIRMATION
I AM READY WILLING AND ABLE TO HEAL,
I AM HEALING

CHARKA
HEART 4
THROAT 5
THIRD EYE 6

HEALING COLOR
GREEN, BLUE, INDIGO

Sit with a straight back. Bring your arms up in front of your throat, fingers spread and outstretched. Connect the thumbs along their length and connect the tips of the pinkies. Bring your hands close to your nose.

BREATH

Inhale deeply and slowly through the nose and then close off the nostrils by placing the thumb tips over them. Hold the breath for as long as you can. Release the thumbs slightly to open the nostrils and exhale. Again hold the breath for as long as possible before inhaling. Repeat the practice for three minutes.

Mudra for Healing
Your Heart Chakra

AFFIRMATION
MY HEART IS LIGHT
AND OPEN TO HAPPINESS

CHAKRA
HEART 4

HEALING COLOR
GREEN

Sit with a straight back. Lift your right hand up, elbow bent, your hand at the level of your face. Make a fist and leave only the index finger extended, pointing up. Place your left hand on your chest above your breast, elbow parallel to the ground. Hold and feel the energy shifting in your body. Keep the elbows nice and high.

BREATH
Long, deep and slow.

Mudra for
Empowering Your Voice

AFFIRMATION
I EXPRESS MYSELF FREELY

CHAKRA
THROAT 5

HEALING COLOR
BLUE

Sit with a straight back. Bend your elbows and hold them parallel to the ground as you bring your hands up in front of you at the level of your throat. Turn the right palm outward and the left palm toward you. Now bend your fingers and hook your hands together, the left hand on the outside. Pull on the hands as if trying to pull them apart, shoulders down.

BREATH
Long, deep and slow.

5. Let Go of Obsession

We have all experienced those frustrating times when an obsessive thought seems to have a strong hold on our mind. No matter how hard you try, the disturbing thought keeps coming back and you feel powerless and unhappy. Perhaps you're worried about something, or you feel angry about an unfortunate incident and can't let go.

For your peace of mind, you must conquer this habit.

Distance yourself from the person who is the object of your anxiety. Remove yourself from the situation that brings you this unease.

Begin your day with this simple routine and practice any of these Mudras anytime during the day when you feel overwhelmed. You will experience immediate relief.

THE FIRST MUDRA will help you release and ease our feelings of worry.

THE SECOND MUDRA will help yo let go of negative emotions connected to your obsessive pattern.

THE THIRD MUDRA will help you command your mind to let go of obsessing so that you can regain peace in your heart and mind.

Mudra for Diminishing Worries

AFFIRMATION
I LET GO OF ALL WORRY AND ANXIETY
I AM WORRY FREE

CHAKRA
HEART 4
THROAT 5
THIRD EYE 6

HEALING COLOR
GREEN, BLUE, INDIGO

Sit with a straight spine. Bring your hands in front of your chest with the palms facing up. The sides of the little fingers and the inner sides of the palms are touching. Now bring your middle fingertips together, perpendicular to the palms. Extend the thumbs away from the palms. Hold and keep the fingers stretched as little antennas for energy.

BREATH
Long, deep and slow.

Mudra for
Releasing Negative Emotions

AFFIRMATION
I RELEASE MY ANGER,
I FEEL PEACE IN MY MIND AND HEART

CHAKRA
HEART 4

HEALING COLOR
GREEN

Sit with a straight spine. Bend your arms and make fists with both hands. Bring them up in front of your heart, left over right. Cross the wrists over each other.

BREATH
Long, deep and slow.

Mudra for Evoking the Power of Jupiter

AFFIRMATION
I COMMAND MY MIND TO STOP OBSESSING,
AND BE AT PEACE

CHAKRA
HEART 4
THROAT 5
THIRD EYE 6

HEALING COLOR
GREEN, BLUE, INDIGO

Sit with a straight spine. Bend the left arm and place the right elbow into the cupped left hand. Make a fist with the right hand and point the index finger up. With the upper part of the right arm, make counterclockwise circles, two revolutions per inhale and two revolutions per exhale. Feel the energy created with your circles.

BREATH
Long, deep and slow.

6. The Analyzing Habit

Some of us have a habit of analyzing and overanalyzing our lives, the lives of others, and every detail in between. We torture ourselves with what-ifs and spend so much time examining every minute of certain events that we take the joy out of the experience. Life does not always make sense and sooner or later you're going to run into a situation that you can focus on as a source of anxiety.

Your nervous system suffers with this habit. You need to stay calm and be still so that you can access the infinite source of knowledge we all possess and find the true answers you are searching for. Most of our anxiety is about not knowing the truth or the future. If you had those answers, would you let go and relax?

This routine will help you overcome the habit so that you can enjoy life's different shades and textures. Let go, trust the universe, and know that all things happen for a reason and it makes no difference or improvement if you analyze it over and over.

Everything is good in moderation and so is analyzing. Let analyzing be a tool instead of a burden that prevents you from enjoying life to the fullest.

THE FIRST MUDRA will immediately help you release anxiety that is the main cause of overanalyzing.

THE SECOND MUDRA will help you soothe and calm the nerves.

THE THIRD MUDRA will help you find the truth you are searching for through meditation. Yu have the capacity to access the universal information bank.
This practice gives you the key.

Mudra for Overcoming Anxiety

AFFIRMATION
I RELEASE ALL ANXIETY AND
WELCOME COMPLETE PEACE

CHAKRA
HEART 4
THROAT 5
THIRD EYE 6

HEALING COLOR
GREEN, BLUE, INDIGO

MANTRA
HARKANAM SAT NAM
(God's Name Is Truth)

Sit with a straight back. Bend your elbows and raise your arms so your upper arms are parallel to the ground and extended out to the sides. Your hands are at the level of your ears, fingers spread wide and pointing up to the sky. Start rotating your hands back and forth, pivoting at the wrists. Practice for three minutes and be persistent. You will go thru a period when it seems difficult, but when you overcome that moment, the practice will become easy. Relax, rest, and enjoy the stillness.

BREATH
Long, deep and strong.

Mudra for Strong Nerves

AFFIRMATION
MY NERVES ARE HEALTHY AND STRONG

CHAKRA
SOLAR PLEXUS 3
HEART 4

HEALING COLOR
YELLOW, GREEN

Sit with a straight spine. Lift your left hand to ear level, palm facing out. Connect the thumb and middle finger and stretch out the other fingers. Place your right hand in front of the solar plexus, palm facing up. The thumb and little fingers are touching while the other fingers are straight.

BREATH

Inhale in four counts and exhale in one strong breath.

Mudra for Finding Perfect Truth

AFFIRMATION
I HAVE KNOWLEDGE
OF THE UNIVERSAL TRUTH

CHAKRA
HEART 4
THROAT 5
THIRD EYE 6
CROWN 7

HEALING COLOR
GREEN, BLUE, INDIGO, VIOLET

MANTRA
SAT NAM
(Truth Is God's Name, One In Spirit)

Sit with a straight spine. Rest both hands on your knees, palms facing up toward the sky. Fingers are together and palms are very lightly cupped. Concentrate on your Third eye and enjoy stillness and peace.

BREATH
Long, deep and slow.

7. Recognize Your Patterns

Surely you have sometimes wondered why you find yourself in a familiar predicament, facing a similar situation that is eerily like one from the past. Maybe you connect with a new partner and face the same old challenging situation.

You may say to yourself you just have bad luck. Or you may face yourself and see it was really you who set up the situation, so you can finally learn your lesson and move on. Recognizing your challenging patterns is a very important step on your journey of self-discovery. A pattern most likely originates in your childhood and it may be useful to retrace the steps back to memories of old experiences. Maybe you were a needy child and now you want too much from your partner.

Maybe your low self-esteem makes you feel you do not deserve better treatment. There are endless possibilities. The essential step is being still with yourself and seeing yourself from a distance with a different perspective. If you were your own best friend, would you see the situation differently? Surely there are times when you tell your friend the truth, which may not be exactly what she expects or wants to hear.

Now you can do that for yourself. It is essential that you spend some time alone without having to defend yourself or your actions to anyone.
Then, have a calm and friendly chat with yourself and be honest.
You may not like all that you see, but no one is perfect so why expect it of yourself?

THE FIRST MUDRA will help you elevate into higher consciousness so that you can recognize your destructive patterns and transform them into positive actions.

THE SECOND MUDRA will help provide a better perception of yourself, your life, your actions, and your interactions. Life is how you look at it. Expand your vision and expand your world.

Mudra for Higher Consciousness

AFFIRMATION
I AM AWARE OF MY LIFE'S LESSONS,
I CAN OVERCOME MY PATTERNS

CHAKRA
SOLAR PLEXUS 3
CROWN -7

HEALING COLOR
YELLOW, VIOLET

Sit with a straight back and lift your hands to solar plexus level with your palms together, fingers pointed away from you. Tuck your thumbs under so that their tips rest on the fleshy mounds below the little fingers. The bottoms of your hands touch firmly and your elbows are to either side.

BREATH
Long, deep and slow.

Mudra for Brain Synchrony-
Readjusting Your Perception

AFFIRMATION
I EXPAND MY VISION AND SEE MYSELF
AND MY LIFE CLEARLY

CHAKRA
THIRD EYE 6
CROWN 7

HEALING COLOR
INDIGO, VIOLET

MANTRA
SA TA NA MA
(Infinity, Birth, Death, Rebirth)

Sit with a straight spine. Make circles with the thumb and index fingers and spread out the rest of the fingers. Lift your arms so your elbows are perpendicular to the ground, hands eye level. Now move your hands toward each other until you can look through the openings in your fingers. As you separate your hands, take a long, slow inhale. As you bring them together in front of your face, exhale long, deep and slow. Repeat.

BREATH
Long, deep with hand movements.

8. Know What You Want

One of the essential ingredients for a fulfilling and happy life is knowing what you want. When you present that question to anyone, carefully pay attention to her or his answer. It will tell you a lot about that person. Now it's your turn.

Ask yourself the same question. If you hear silence and can not give yourself an answer, it is time to do some soul searching.

You may be superbly talented, a hard worker, and a lovely human being, but if you do not know what you want, life will be difficult.

If you don't know what you want, you certainly won't get it. Or even worse, you won't know it when you do get it.

Inner searching and reflection are necessary for you to remember the reasons you came into this life. The answer may be simple, and knowing it will give you a tremendous sense of belonging and inner satisfaction.

Know yourself and you will become a complete human being.

THE FIRST MUDRA will help you reach into your memory treasure chest for the essential information about why you are here.

THE SECOND MUDRA will help you fulfill your desires.

THE THIRD MUDRA will connect you with the knowledge of your life's mission and your destined assignments.

Mudra for Concentration

AFFIRMATION
WHAT I WANT IS CLEAR TO ME

CHAKRA
Solar plexus 3
Heart 4
Crown 7

HEALING COLOR
Yellow, green, violet

MANTRA
AKAL AKAL AKAL HARI AKAL
(Immortal Creator)

Sit with a straight spine. Bend your elbows and bring your arms to your chest. Each thumb and index finger should form a circle. The index finger is curled far into the beginning of the thumb. The other fingers are stretched up. Connect your hands and outstretched fingers back to back. Be still, concentrate on your Third Eye.

BREATH
Long, deep and slow.

Mudra for Efficiency

AFFIRMATION
I HAVE A PRECISE PLAN OF ACTION
TO HELP FULFILL MY DESIRES

CHAKRA
HEART 4
THIRD EYE 6

HEALING COLOR
GREEN, INDIGO

MANTRA
ATMA PARMATMA GURU HARI
(Soul, Supreme Soul, the Teacher in His Supreme Power and Wisdom)

Sit with a straight back and bring your arms up in front of your heart, the palms turned in toward you. The palm of the right hand is placed outside the left. All fingers are straight. The thumb tips are pressed firmly together and the forearms are parallel to the ground. Breathe and take your time. Relax and be still.

BREATH
Inhale slowly and deeply, hold for ten honest seconds,
and exhale for ten seconds.

Mudra for Receiving God's Law

AFFIRMATION
MY LIFE'S MISSION IS VERY CLEAR TO ME,
I AM READY AND HONORED
TO FULFILL MY LIFE'S MISSION

CHAKRA
CROWN -7

HEALING COLOR
VIOLET

MANTRA
OM
(God in His Absolute State)

Sit with a straight back. Lift the right hand to heart level, palm facing down, and the left hand to your solar plexus area, palm facing up toward the sky. Leave enough space between the palms for a small ball. Elbows are to the side. All fingers are together and straight. Hold the Mudra and concentrate on the energy between your palms.

BREATH
Long, deep and slow.

9. Positive Thoughts Make a Positive Life

Thoughts are like radio signals or electricity. They are very fine vibrations permeating the ether. When a positive thought is directed with intention to someone else, it will be felt and it will affect them positively.

When faced with difficult situations or people, visualize surrounding them in white light and send them love. You will be amazed at the quick and powerful results. Your minds extremely complex tool and a positive outlook on life will make your life positive. Do not let the negativity of others affect you.

Be selective about your environment and the people with whom you keep company so as to keep your immediate environment clear of negativity. Everything around you is affected by your thought vibrations. Cooking a meal with love will permeate it with the vibration of love. Starting the day with a positive frame of mind will give you and entirely new outlook. Make an effort to live every moment with a positive frame of mind. Seeing the good in everything will transform others around you and eventually our world will be filled with peace, harmony, and love.

THE FIRST MUDRA will help you recognize negative environments and people so that you can distance yourself from unhealthy situations.

THE SECOND MUDRA will help you remove negative forces that have been keeping you stuck in unpleasant situations so that you may move into a more positive space.

THE THIRD MUDRA will help you develop self-confidence so that you may erase self-doubt and feel positive in all areas of your life.

Mudra for
Taking You Out of Danger

AFFIRMATION
I AM PROTECTED AND ALL IS WELL

CHAKRA
ALL

HEALING COLOR
ALL

MANTRA
GUROO GUROO WAHAY GUROO,
GUROO RAAM DAS GUROO
(As a Servant of the Infinite I Receive His Wisdom)

Sit with a straight spine and raise your arms so that your hands are on either side of your face. Curl your fingers into fists, except for the thumbs, which should point gently toward the sky. Continue holding for at least three minutes.

BREATH
Long, deep and slow.

Mudra for
Taking Away Hardships

AFFIRMATION
I AM REMOVING ALL OBSTACLES,
MY ROAD TO PROSPERITY IS FREE

CHAKRA
THIRD EYE 6
CROWN 7

HEALING COLOR
INDIGO, VIOLET

MANTRA
HAR HARE GOBINDAY, HAR HARE MUKUNDAY
(He Is My Sustainer, He Is My Liberator)

Sit with a straight spine and make fists with both hands, keeping the thumbs on the outside. Now swing your arms in big circles, like a pendulum. Begin with a movement forward and up, then go back and down. Repeat for three minutes.

BREATH
Long, deep and slow.

Mudra for Self-Confidence

AFFIRMATION
I BELIEVE IN MYSELF AND KNOW
THAT I CAN ACCOMPLISH ANYTHING I DESIRE

CHAKRA
SOLAR PLEXUS 3
THIRD EYE 6

HEALING COLOR
YELLOW, INDIGO

MANTRA
EK ONG KAR SAT GURU PRASAD,
SAT GURU PRASAD EK ONG KAR
(The Creator Is the One That Dispels Darkness and Illuminates Us by His Grace)

Sit with a straight spine. Lift your hands up to the level of your solar plexus with elbows bent to the sides. Bend the middle, ring, and little fingers and touch them back to back. Extend the index fingers and thumbs and press them together. The thumbs are pointed toward you and the index fingers away from you.

BREATH
Long, deep and slow.

Part Four

I Sing with My Soul

This life's journey is only a drop in the ocean of your soul's infinite path.

Remember that you are an immortal being having an Earthly experience.

Enjoy it, appreciate its textures, and act accordingly to your higher knowledge of truth, love, and goodness.

Radiate these qualities to everyone you meet on your path and know that a smile can touch a person's heart, open their mind, and remind them of the pure love and light that is the essence of all souls.

1. Open Your Heart to Love

Are you ready for love? Some of us seem to talk about it for years and yet when love appears at our doorstep we run the other way.

Self-love is an essential step in your readiness for a loving relationship.

Spend some time with yourself, and really get to know who you are.

Do you like what you see? It is never too late for improvement.
How you feel about yourself will influence how your partner sees you as well.
Are you in love because he/she is accepting of who you are and makes you feel loved, something that you can not give yourself?

Being loving to yourself will help you attract a loving and harmonious partner.

THE FIRST MUDRA will help you open your heart to yourself. Knowing what is inside your heart is the key to your understanding of who you are and what you desire. If your heart is filled with tears, let them out and replace them with peace and tranquility.

THE SECOND MUDRA will help you empower the love in your heart so that you may attract a loving partner into your life. Like attracts like.

THE THIRD MUDRA will help you reconnect with the source of all love - the Divine power within.

Mudra for Opening Your Heart

AFFIRMATION
I OPEN MY HEART,
I RELEASE ALL SORROW,
AND REPLACE IT WITH
THE PURE LIGHT OF LOVE

CHAKRA
HEART 4

HEALING COLOR
GREEN

Sit with a straight spine. Bend your elbows and lift your hands up in front of your chest. The palms are looking up toward the sky and all fingers are spread apart. The hands are not touching. Keep the fingers stretched out as antennas of energy. Visualize your open heart filled with glowing healing green or rose pink light.

BREATH
Long, deep and slow.

Mudra for Love

AFFIRMATION
I FILL MY HEART WITH LOVE
AND AM READY
TO GIVE AND RECEIVE LOVE

CHAKRA
HEART 6

HEALING COLOR
GREEN

MANTRA
SAT NAM WAHE GURU
(God Is Truth, His Is the Supreme Power and Wisdom)

Sit with a straight spine and raise your hands to either side of your head. Curl the middle and ring fingers into your palms and extend the thumbs, index fingers, and little fingers. Keep your elbows from sinking as you hold for three minutes.

BREATH
Inhale eight short counts, with one strong, long exhale.

Mudra for Divine Worship

AFFIRMATION
I REPLENISH MY HEART
WITH THE DIVINE UNIVERSAL POWER
THAT IS THE SOURCE OF ALL LOVE

CHAKRA
ALL

HEALING COLOR
ALL

MANTRAEK ONG KAR
(One Creator, God Is One)

Sit with a straight spine. Place your palms together in front of your chest. Sit still and concentrate on your Third Eye for at least three minutes.

BREATH
Long, deep and strong.

2. See Into Your Future

Remember when you were a little girl and you wanted to know about your future?
Where will I be, who will I be, and how will I look?
Will I be beautiful, will I be happy, and will my Prince Charming come?

Today you have the answers to some of those questions, but not all of them. And the little girl in you still wonders what will happen.

It is possible to get the answers when you learn to listen to your intuitive voice. Deep in your psyche you know your potential future and it is important to remember that gift we all have been given.

Nothing is written in stone; you always have options that are connected to your everyday choices. Your destiny has variables and with awareness you can help turn your life and the lives of others toward exciting and positive directions.
With this specific practice you will open and activate the centers that have the data you wish to access.

It is important to take time, be patient, and really learn to be still and quiet.
Only then will you be able to hear your inner voice.

THE FIRST MUDRA will activate, energize, and help open your higher chakras.
THE SECOND MUDRA will help you find the guidance you are asking for.
THE THIRD MUDRA will deepen your capacity for insight into your future. Listen carefully, be still, and keep it simple.
Ask a clear, simple question and you will receive a clear, simple answer.
That is all you need.

Mudra for Your Upper Centers

AFFIRMATION
I SEND VITAL ENERGY TO MY UPPER CHAKRAS
SO THAT I MAY BE OPEN
AND CONNECTED TO THE DIVINE

CHAKRA
THROAT 5
THIRD EYE 6
CROWN 7

HEALING COLOR
BLUE, INDIGO, VIOLET

MANTRA
SAT NAM
(Truth Is God's Name, One in Spirit)

Sit with a straight back and place your fists on your knees palms up. Curl your fingers into fists, except for the thumbs, which are stretched out and pointed away from you, parallel to the ground. Concentrate on recharging and feel the energy in your thumbs activate your higher centers. Hold for three minutes and relax.

BREATH
Long, deep and strong.

Mudra for Guidance

AFFIRMATION
I ASK FOR GUIDANCE ...
I POSE A SIMPLE QUESTION
AND I WAIT FOR A CLEAR ANSWER

CHAKRA
CROWN 7

HEALING COLOR
VIOLET

MANTRA
SAT NAM
(Truth Is God's Name, One in Spirit)

Sit with a straight spine. Bring your hands together at chest level as if forming a cup. The palms are facing up and the sides of the little fingers are pressed together. Focus your eyes past the tip of your nose toward your hands. Be still, holding and concentrating on your breath.

BREATH
Long, slow, and deep breath into the palms of your hands.

Mudra for Powerful Insight

AFFIRMATION
I DEEPEN MY INSIGHT
AND EXPAND MY VISION
INTO THE REALMS OF TIMELESSNESS

CHAKRA
THIRD EYE 6

HEALING COLOR
INDIGO

MANTRA
SAT NAM
(Truth Is God's Name, One in Spirit)

Sit with a straight spine. Bend your elbows and raise your hands to the level of the navel. Make a gentle fist with your left hand and place it palm side up into the palm of your right hand. Cross your thumbs, left over right. Concentrate on your Third Eye, breathe, and hold for three minutes.

BREATH
Long, deep and slow.

3. Create Your Dream

As a child you probably had many dreams. They were simple, but to you they meant the world. You have achieved many of your dreams, and there are most likely some you've given up on. Have you thought abut your dreams lately?

Try to remember your childhood dreams. What was your favorite thing to do when you were nine years old? Did you have any special hobbies? You'll be surprised what you'll remember. It will help you realize how many of your dreams did come true. It is important to always have dreams. As life changes, so do your dreams. Be content and grateful for the dreams that came true and don't let the unfulfilled dreams bring you down. Look at them from another perspective and see if different approach to acquiring them may be helpful. Be realistic and go about it patiently, with a tangible plan.

Dreams can be your reality, if you know what they are. Speak out loud and let your friends know what you desire. That is the first step. Keeping dreams to yourself will keep them unrealized. If you don't dare to voice them, how will you dare to live them?

When you share your dreams, you may hear helpful input and "by coincidence" the next step will reveal itself. Remember that all you desires are there for a reason. They are meant to remind you about fulfilling your destiny and your mission. So revive your dreams, follow them, and know that your dreams can and will become your reality.

THE FIRST MUDRA will help you with opening, activating, and recharging your creative center.

THE SECOND MUDRA will help you achieve a positive outlook about life and a happy disposition where dreams are created.

THE THIRD MUDRA will help you connect to the inner voice of your soul, so that your dreams will be in harmony with your life's purpose.

Mudra for Second Chakra

AFFIRMATION
I AM OPENING AND ACTIVATING
MY CENTER OF CREATIVE ENERGY

CHAKRA
REPRODUCTIVE ORGANS 2

HEALING COLOR
ORANGE

MANTRA
SAT NAM
(Truth Is God's Name, One in Spirit)

Sit with a straight spine and bring your hands up to just below the throat. Cup your hands with palms up. The pinkies and thumbs are outstretched while the other three fingers are held together. The sides of little fingers are touching, and the thumbs are separated and pointing toward your body. Hold for three minutes.

BREATH
Long, deep and slow.

Mudra for Happiness

AFFIRMATION
I SEE MYSELF HAPPY, HEALTHY,
AND IMMEASURABLY BLESSED

CHAKRA
HEART 4

HEALING COLOR
GREEN

MANTRA
SAT NAM
(Truth Is God's Name, One in Spirit)

Sit with a straight spine. Bend your elbows and bring your arms to your sides, away from your body. Elbows are just below the level of the shoulders. Palms are facing forward. Stretch the index and middle fingers and bend the ring and little fingers, pressing them into the palms firmly with the thumbs. Hold for three minutes and relax.

BREATH
Long, deep and slow.

Mudra for Creativity

AFFIRMATION
I HAVE ACCESS TO THE INFINITE
CREATIVE POTENTIAL OF THIS UNIVERSE
ALL I CREATE IS
FOR THE GOODNESS OF THIS WORLD

CHAKRA
THIRD EYE 6
CROWN 7

HEALING COLOR
INDIGO, VIOLET

MANTRA
GA DA
(God)

Sit with a straight spine. Connect the thumbs and index fingers, keeping the rest of the fingers straight. Bend your elbows and lift your hands to your sides with palms facing up at a sixty-degree angle to your body. Concentrate on your Third Eye center and meditate for at least three minutes.

BREATH
Short, fast breath or fire from the navel.

4. Embrace Your Friendships

Where would we be without our dear friends? Sometimes we forget the necessity of bonding with female friends and not competing with them. We are in this life together and in this world at the same chosen time. Helping each other through our challenges as well as our joys is what sharing the human experience is all about. Friendships with members of the opposite sex also have special qualities that are extremely important for our broader vision, understanding, and acceptance of human relationships. When you surround yourself with only female friends, you're missing a very beneficial male perspective.

Don't forget that we are in this world together. In order to avoid conflicts, pay attention to your actions, your expectations, and you sensitivity to others.

When a disharmony occurs, make an effort to clear the air and preserve the friendship. With some inner reflection and time you can resolve the conflict objectively. Keep in mind that there are times when friendships change; we ourselves are constantly changing. Maybe you have less in common and life's path takes you in different directions. Keep an open mind and many times an old friend from the past may return and reconnect with you again later in life.

And never forget to be a good friend yourself.
What you give to others in friendship will come back to you tenfold.

THE FIRST MUDRA will help you see yourself objectively so that the friendship you offer is giving and loving, which in return will attract the same to you.
THE SECOND MUDRA will help you connect with the energies of this world so that you will magnetically attract friends who vibrate at the same loving level of your heart.
THE THIRD MUDRA will help you keep a steady flow of energy toward your friendships so that they may last eternally in harmony.

Mudra for Stronger Character

AFFIRMATION
I LOOK AT MYSELF FROM AFAR
AND SEE CLEARLY AND OBJECTIVELY
THE QUALITIES I REFLECT
AND SHARE WITH THE WORLD

CHAKRA
SOLAR PLEXUS 3
THIRD EYE 6

HEALING COLOR
YELLOW, INDIGO

MANTRA
HUMME HUM BRAHAM
(Calling on the Infinite Self)

Sit with a straight spine, hold your hands in relaxed fists at your sides. Thumbs are on the outside and index fingers are straight and pointing up. Lift your left hand to chin level and your right hand slightly higher, palms facing each other. Hold, keeping your eyes open and looking forward.

BREATH
Long, deep and slow.

Mudra for Calling the Gods of the Earth

AFFIRMATION
I CALL TO THE GODS OF THE EARTH
TO SEND OLD FRIENDS MY WAY

CHAKRA
BASE OF SPINE 1
CROWN 7

HEALING COLOR
RED, VIOLET

MANTRA
OM
(God in His Absolute State)

Sit with a straight spine. Bend your elbows and place your left hand at your solar plexus, palm facing upward, fingers together. Bring your right hand below your left, palm facing your body, and point the right index finger down toward the Earth.

BREATH
Long, deep and slow.

Mudra for
Universal Energy and Eternity

AFFIRMATION
I EMBRACE, CHERISH, AND NURTURE
MY FRIENDSHIPS NOW
AND FOREVER

CHAKRA
BASE OF SPINE 1
CROWN 7

HEALING COLOR
RED, VIOLET

MANTRA
HAR HARE HAREE WAHE GURU
*(God, the Creator of Supreme Power and Wisdom,
the Spiritual Teacher and Guide Through Darkness)*

Sit with a straight spine and bend your elbows, bring your hands up and away from your body so as to form two V's. Raise your palms to just below your heart level, with fingers close together. Be still and feel the energy flowing into your hands.

BREATH
Long, deep and strong.

5. Let Go of the Past

Life is full of ups and downs and we all have our share of pain and sorrow.

We can learn from those experiences so that we can avoid them in the future. We can also share our experiences with others and help them get through challenges with less trouble. There is always a positive aspect to difficult life challenges. Many life-altering events occur when you are forced to change because the pain is too deep. Once you get through the hurricane it is time to move on and be open for new, happy events.

Hanging on to the past only takes up valuable space in your memory bank that is needed for positive and creative energy. Holding on becomes a comfort zone that prevents us from experiencing the new.

It is up to you to release old negative emotions and make room for the new you.

THE FIRST MUDRA will help you release any fears and anger that may be lingering in your Third Chakra-solar plexus area.

THE SECOND MUDRA will help you heal your heart and release the sorrow you may be carrying with you.

THE THIRD MUDRA will help you trust the universal creative forces that a brighter day is ahead for you and happiness is at your fingertips.

Mudra for Third Chakra

AFFIRMATION
I RELEASE ALL THE HURT,
AND ANGER FROM THE PAST
AND MAKE SPACE
FOR NEW, HAPPY EVENTS

CHAKRA
SOLAR PLEXUS 3

HEALING COLOR
YELLOW

MANTRA
SAT NAM
(Truth Is God's Name, One in Spirit)

Sit with a straight back. Bend your elbows and lift your hands up, elbows parallel to the ground. The palms are facing forward, all fingers together, except for the thumbs, which are pointing toward the ears. Hold and keep the elbows nice and high for three minutes.

BREATH

Short, fast breath of fire from the navel.

Mudra for
Help with a Grave Situation

AFFIRMATION
I RELEASE ALL SORROW FROM MY HEART
AND AM OPEN FOR LOVE AND PASSION
TO FLOW INTO MY LIFE AND HEART

CHAKRA
HEART 4

HEALING COLOR
GREEN

MANTRA
HUMME HUM, BRAHAM HUM, BRAHAM HUM
(Calling upon Your Infinite Self)

Sit with a straight spine. Bend your elbows and place both palms on your upper chest, fingers pointing toward each other. Hold and feel the healing energy of your hands soothe the heart.

BREATH
Long, deep and strong.

Mudra for Trust

AFFIRMATION
I TRUST IN THE UNIVERSAL CREATOR
THAT ALL GOOD THINGS AND EXPERIENCES
ARE COMING MY WAY

CHAKRA
CROWN 7

HEALING COLOR
VIOLET

MANTRA
HAR HAR HAR WAHE GURU
(God's Creation, His Supreme Power and Wisdom)

Sit with a straight spine. Make a circle with you arms arched up and over your head. Place the right palm on top of the left. Press the thumb tips together and visualize a protective circle of white light that surrounds you.

BREATH
Short, fast breath of fire from navel.

6. Know Yourself

Know yourself and you will know the world. Isn't it interesting how many of us have a solution for all the problems of the world and yet when it comes to ourselves we can't answer the simplest questions?

You have to spend time with yourself to know who you are. Are you paying attention to your needs, dreams, wishes, and desires?
Do you know your body, when it really needs to rest, and what it needs to be nourished with? Do you hear your mind when it's sending you signals and warnings or are you just ignoring it? Do you know the true reasons for having repeated difficulties in personal relationships or finding your life's mission?

You may be attracting partners who are confronting you with unresolved issues of your past. Get to know your true self. If you face these issues yourself you will crate a space for a new harmonious relationship. Go for a walk in nature, rest when your body is tired, and learn to spend a few minutes a day in stillness and silence without distractions. Talk to yourself like your own best friend. If you carry within you feelings of discontent, ask yourself what would make you happy.

What do you need to do to get there? Make a list. Know that you will be of better help to others if and when you are content with yourself. The answer might be quite simple.
And you will discover what a lovely, happy, and positive person you are.

THE FIRST MUDRA will help you get into the routine of sitting still with yourself and meditating.
THE SECOND MUDRA will help you honestly assess your behavior.
THE THIRD MUDRa will help you explore your intuitive vision and find answers to your deep, old, and maybe unresolved questions.

Mudra for Developing Meditation

AFFIRMATION
I FEEL THE BEAT OF THE UNIVERSE IN MYSELF
I AM CONNECTED
TO THE UNIVERSAL CREATIVE POWER

CHAKRA
ALL

HEALING COLOR
ALL

MANTRA
SAT NAM
(Truth Is God's Name, One in Spirit)

Sit with a straight spine. With the four fingers of your right hand feel the pulse on your left wrist. Press lightly and feel the pulse in each fingertip. Close your eyes and concentrate on your Third ye. With each beat of your pulse, mentally repeat the mantra.

BREATH
Long, deep and strong.

Mudra for Inner Integrity

AFFIRMATION
I SEE MYSELF AND MY HABITS CLEARLY.
I TAKE RESPONSIBILITY
FOR ALL MY ACTIONS
I AM READY TO CONQUER
MY INNER FEARS

CHAKRA
THROAT 5
THIRD EYE 6

HEALING COLOR
BLUE, INDIGO

MANTRA
SAT NAM
(Truth Is God's Name, One in Spirit)

Sit with a straight back. Bend your elbows and lift your upper arms parallel to the ground. Bring your hands to ear level, palms facing out. Curl your fingers inward and point the thumbs out toward your ears. Hold for three minutes and relax.

BREATH
Short, fast breath of fire from navel.

Mudra for Sixth Chakra - Truth

AFFIRMATION
I INTUITIVELY KNOW WHY I AM HERE
AND WHAT MY LIFE PURPOSE IS,
WHAT I NEED TO KNOW
WILL BE REVEALED NOW

CHAKRA
THIRD EYE 6

HEALING COLOR
INDIGO

MANTRA
EK ONG KAR
(One Creator, God Is One)

Sit with a straight back. Bend your elbows and lift your arms up to so that the elbows are parallel to the ground. Palms are facing out and all fingers are together. Hold for three minutes and concentrate on your Third Eye.

BREATH
Long, deep and slow.

7. Be Nice to Yourself

You are setting and example of how you want to be treated by how you treat yourself. Love, respect, listen to, and be nice to yourself and others will be as well.

It is important to be aware of our environment and the people in it. They may be inharmonious to our nature. When you sense that your energy is drained by those around you, find a quiet corner and "make yourself invisible".

Be protective and good to yourself, and you'll be amazed how quickly your situation will improve. Have a daily ritual of treating yourself.

A few moments of time alone in the morning is a gift to yourself for a happy and peaceful day. In the evening you can treat yourself to a candlelight bath, a cup of tea while listening to soft relaxing music, or sitting outdoors and consciously breathing for at least three minutes. Simple acts of kindness will let your inner psyche know that you care about yourself and thus you will attract people who care about you.

Others will admire your capacity for self-love and will want to participate.
Set an example and share the joy of self-love.

THE FIRST MUDRA will help you "become invisible" when your environment is draining you.
THE SECOND MUDRA will help you protect yourself from daily stress.
THE THIRD MUDRA will help you feel content and cozy so that your inner self feels rewarded and acknowledged for all the hard work of being you.

Mudra for Invisibility

AFFIRMATION
I AM INVISIBLE
TO ALL NEGATIVE FORCES AROUND ME
AND I AM PROTECTED
AND TAKEN CARE OF

CHAKRA
ALL

HEALING COLOR
ALL

MANTRA
OM
(God in His Absolute State)

Sit with a straight spine and make a fist with your right hand. Lift it to the level of your solar plexus, the palm facing toward you. Now hold your left hand above your right fist, palm facing down. The hands are not touching. Hold for three minutes and relax.

BREATH
Long, deep and slow.

Mudra for Preventing Stress

AFFIRMATION
I AM SERENE, PEACEFUL, AND RELAXED

CHAKRA
SOLAR PLEXUS 3

HEALING COLOR
YELLOW

Sit with a straight back. Bend your elbows and bring your forearms in front of your solar plexus area parallel to the ground. Rest the back of the left hand in the palm of the right hand, both palms facing up. Fingers are straight and together. Hold for three minutes and concentrate on your breath.

BREATH
Long, deep and strong.

Mudra for Contentment

AFFIRMATION
I AM CONTENT WITH MY LIFE
I AM DOING WONDERFULLY

CHARKA
SOLAR PLEXUS 3

HEALING COLOR
YELLOW

MaANTRA
SARE SA SA SARE SA SA SARE HARE HAR
(God is Infinite in His Creativity)

Sit with a straight back and lift your hands in front of your stomach area. Connect the thumb and the middle finger of the right hand and the thumb and the little finger of the left hand. Relax the rest of the fingers and hold your hands a few inches apart, palms up. Hold for three minutes, then make fists with both hands and relax.

BREATH
Long, deep and slow.

8. Learn to Say No

Are you a people pleaser?

Always available for everyone else's convenience and making sure that everyone is happy and content?

Those can be great qualities, but know the healthy limitations. What about you?

When you are sacrificing your own peace, happiness and health to run around and please everyone else, it is time to look at yourself.

You have no one else to blame but the person you see in the mirror. Take a deep breath and ask yourself whether you really want to do what you're promising you will, or want to go somewhere where you're asked to go.

It is very important and self-empowering to be able to say: "No, I do not want to do this at this moment. I need time for yourself."

Give it a try. It may be difficult in the beginning, but after a while you will feel better and be better company for others and yourself. Every time you find yourself in this predicament, practice this routine. It will help you achieve that wonderful state of self-empowerment in which you do things for others without compromising and forgetting yourself.

THE FIRST MUDRA will help you protect yourself from people who drain your energy and from your own susceptible nature to please everybody.

THE SECOND MUDRA will help you with making wise choices and being selective about when you do something for someone else.

Mudra for Protection

AFFIRMATION
I PROTECT MYSELF
FROM ALL PEOPLE
WHO TAKE MORE THAN THEY GIVE.
I SURROUND MYSELF
WITH GIVING AND LOVING FRIENDS

CHAKRA
ALL

HEALING COLOR
ALL

MANTRA
OM
(God in His Absolute State)

Sit with a straight spine. Cross your left hand over your right one and place them on your upper chest. Palms are facing you and all fingers are together. Hold for three minutes and feel the immediate energy shift.

BREATH
Long, deep and slow.

Mudra for Wisdom

AFFIRMATION
I CALL ON MY HIGHER KNOWLEDGE
TO HELP ME CHOOSE WISELY
WHEN I OFFER MY HELP

CHAKRA
SOLAR PLEXUS 3
HEART 4
CROWN 7

HEALING COLOR
YELLOW, GREEN, VIOLET

MANTRA
SAT NAM
(Truth Is God's Name, One in Spirit)

Sit with a straight spine and bend your elbows to the side, parallel to the ground. Make gentle fists, with the thumbs inside and the index fingers out. Now hook your index fingers around each other. The right palm is facing down and the left toward your chest.

BREATH
Long, deep and slow.

9. Yes, You Deserve

Have you ever noticed an unease when getting a compliment, or receiving a gift?

You may dismiss the compliment entirely just because you are incapable of accepting such a simple gift. And you may always make sure you tell everyone you do not want any gifts for your birthday, just so you won't be disappointed in case you are forgotten. Go back in time and unravel your past with gifts.

Where you ever rewarded as a child? Did you receive praise or criticism?
Maybe a critical voice of the past is following you to the present.

What about when all is really great in your life but maybe not in your friend's? You suddenly feel guilty and undeserving of the good fortune and happiness bestowed upon you. You might even sabotage or decline your gifts in life because of it. Maybe you fear every day that your lucky and happy life will be gone in an instant.

You deserve the best. Know your birthright for love, happiness, health, and prosperity. Work hard, make an effort, and then patiently pay attention to which destined door opens. Enter, enjoy your deserved good fortune, and make the best of it.
It may not be according to your plan, but maybe a much better one.

THE FIRST MUDRA will help you acknowledge that you deserve all you strive for and work hard for. Voice your wishes and praise out loud, even if just to yourself.
THE SECOND MUDRA will evoke your given powers to prosper physically, emotionally, and materially.
THE THIRD MUDRA will help you achieve success and victory in all your endeavors to help yourself, your loved ones, and all humankind. When the intentions are positive and helpful to others, you will be rewarded with good fortune.

Mudra for Fifth Chakra

AFFIRMATION
I DESERVE LOVE, RESPECT, AND KINDNESS
I DESERVE HEALTH, HAPPINESS,
AND PROSPERITY
NOW AND ALWAYS

CHAKRA
THROAT 5

HEALING COLOR
BLUE

MANTRA
EK ONG KAR
(One Creator, God Is One)

Sit with a straight back and bend your elbows, lifting them up parallel to the ground. Make fists with both hands, leaving the index fingers pointing straight up. Bring your hands up to either side of your head, palm facing you. Hold and be aware of the energy shift in your fingers.

BREATH
Long, deep and slow.

Mudra for Prosperity

AFFIRMATION
I AM PROSPEROUS PHYSICALLY, EMOTIONALLY, AND

CHAKRA
BASE OF SPINE 1
REPRODUCTIVE ORGANS 2
SOLAR PLEXUS 3

HEALING COLOR
RED, ORANGE, YELLOW

MANTRA
HAR HAR
(God, God)

Sit with a straight spine. Bring your hands in front of you, fingers together and palms facing down. Press the sides of the index fingers together and hold for a second. Now turn your hands over so that the palms are facing up toward the sky for a second and the edges of the little fingers are touching. Keep repeating and chant the mantra HAR with each change of hand position. Continue the practice for eleven minutes and rest.

BREATH
Short, fast breath of fire from the point of the navel, repeated with each mantra and fast Mudra movement.

Mudra for Victory

AFFIRMATION
I AM VICTORIOUS IN HELPING MYSELF,
OTHERS, AND OUR WORLD
TO BECOME A HAPPY, HEALTHY,
AND PEACEFUL HOME

CHAKRA
ALL

HEALING COLOR
ALL

MANTRA
OM
(God in His Absolute State)

Sit with a straight spine. Make gentle fists with both hands and cross them in front of your upper chest, left over right. This Mudra is seen in many sculptures of pharaohs in Egypt.

BREATH
Long, deep and slow.

Ten Rules of a True Goddess of Nature

1. Strength

My delicate yet strong feminine power resides within my soul.
I claim it, teach it, and share it with the rest of the world.

2. Assignment

I have chosen my assignments in this life.
I remember to enjoy, and honor them.
I remember the assignment of just being me.

3. Power

My power is not measured by size, quantity and material riches.
It is the power of my soul, being a part of the ultimate creative
Divine energy that guides me through birth and my life's challenges.

4. Love

I surround myself with love
that extends to all beings in this world
and the entire Universe.

5. Compassion

I am nonjudgmental and compassionate and embrace all beings.

6. Generosity

What I give, I shall receive.
Giving from the heart touches and awakens
the giving spirit and brings a smile to someone's face.

7. Self-Respect

I respect my own body, mind, and spirit.
I teach others to respect themselves,
and the ultimate creative power of the Universe.

8. Vision

The power of my mind needs my reins
to help my life journey go where my heart desires.

9. Healing

My loving smile and touch can heal this world.

10. Illumination

Being a Light force, I pay attention to my power
I share my bright Light with the world.
I inspire and guide others in time of darkness and doubt.
I nourish my essence with nature.
I am a glorious part of this world.
This is my life purpose.

Mantras Pronunciation Guide

SOUND VIBRATIONS THAT ELEVATE YOUR SPIRIT

A like the **a** in **about**

AA like the **a** in **want**

AY like the **ay** in **say**

AI like the **a** in **sand**

I like the **i** in **bit**

U like the **u** in **put**

OO like the **oo** in **good**

O like the **o** in **no**

E like the **ay** in **say**

EE like the **e** in **meet**

AAU like the **ow** in **now**

SAT rhymes with "**what**"

NAM rhymes with "**mom**"

WAHE - sounds like "**wa-hay**"

GU- sounds luke "**put**"

Emphasize the *ch* at the end of every "**such**"

Pronounce the consonant **v** softly

Roll the **r**'s slightly

When chanting a mantra like "**Haree Har Haree Har,**"
make sure you do not move your lips,
and pronounce it with tongue only.

Mudra for Inner Security

AD SHAKTI AD SHAKTI

(I bow to the Creator's Power)

Mudra for Concentration

AKAL AKAL AKAL HARI AKAAL

(Immortal Creator)

Mudra for Efficiency

ATMA PARMATMA GURU HARI

(Soul, Supreme Soul, the Teacher in His Supreme Power and Wisdom)

Mudra for Divine Worship

EK ONG KAR

(One Creator, God Is One)

Mudra for Patience

EK ONG KAR SAT GURU PRASAAD

(One Creator, Illuminated by God's Grace)

Mudra for Anti-Aging

EK ONG KAR SA TA NA MA

(One Creator of Infinity, Birth, Death, and Rebirth)

Mudra for Self-Confidence

EK ONG KAR SAT GURU PRASAD
SAT GURU PRASAD EK ONG KAR
(The creator Is the One That Dispels Darkness and Illuminates us by His Grace)

Mudra for Creativity

GA DA
(God)

Mudra for Mental Balance

GOBINDAY, MUKUNDAY, UDAARAY, APAARAY,
HARYNG, KARYNG, NIRNAAMAY, AKAAMAY
(Sustainer, Liberator, Enlightener, Infinite, Destroyer, Creator, Nameless, Desireless)

Mudra to Take You Out of Danger

GUROO GUROO WAHAY GUROO,
GUROO RAAM DAS GUROO
(As a Servant of the Infinite I Receive His Wisdom)

Mudra for Prosperity

HAR HAR
(God, God)

Mudra for Trust

HAR HAR HAR WAHE GURU
(God's Creation, His Supreme Power and Wisdom)

Mudra for Eternity

HAR HARE HAREE WAHE GURU
(God the Creator of Supreme Power and Wisdom, the Spiritual Teacher and Guide through Darkness)

Mudra for Releasing Anxiety

HARKANAM SAT NAM
(God's Name Is Truth)

Mudra for Taking Away Hardships

HAR HAR GOBINDAY HAR HARE MUKUNDAY
(He Is My Sustainer, He Is My Liberator)

Mudra for Relaxation and Joy

HAREE HAR HAREE HAR
(God in His Creative Aspect)

Mudra for Help in a Grave Situation

HUMME HUM, BRAHAM HUM, BRAHAM HUM
(Calling upon Your Infinite Self)

Mudra for Stronger Character

HUMME HUM BRAHAM
(Calling on the Infinite Self)

Mudra for Tranquilizing the Mind

MAN HAR TAN HAR GURU HAR

(Mind with God, Soul with God, the Divine Guide and His Supreme Wisdom)

Mudra for Facing Fear

NIRBHAO NIRVAIR AKAAL MORT

(Fearless, Without Enemy, Immortal Personified God)

Mudra for Rejuvenation

OM

(God in His Absolute State)

Mudra for Powerful Energy

OOOOONG

(God as Creator in Manifestation)

Mudra for Change

ONG NAMEO GURU DEV NAMO

(I Bow to the Infinity of the Creator,
I Call on the Infinite Creative Consciousness and Divine Wisdom)

Mudra for Better Communication

RAA MAA

(I am Balance Between the Sun and the Moon, the Earth and the Ether)
RA(the Sun energy, generating force)
MA (the Moon Energy, receptive force)

Mudra for Wisdom

SAT NAM

(Truth Is God's Name, One in Spirit)

Mudra for Creativity

SARE SA SA SARE SA SA SARE HARE HAR

(God Is Infinite in His Creativity)

Mudra of Love

SAT NAM WAHE GURU

(God Is Truth, His Is the Supreme Power and Wisdom)

Mudra for Adjusting Your Perception

SA TA NA MA

(Infinity, Birth, Death, Rebirth)

ABOUT THE AUTHOR

SABRINA MESKO Ph.D.H. is a recognized Mudra authority and International and Los Angeles Times bestselling author of the timeless classic *Healing Mudras - Yoga for your Hands* translated into fourteen languages. She authored over twenty books on Mudras, Mudra Therapy, Mudras and Astrology, and meditation techniques.

Sabrina was born in Europe where she became a classical ballerina at an early age. In her teens she moved to New York and became a principal Broadway dancer and singer who turned to yoga to heal a back injury. Easter-trained but Western-based, she completed a several-year intensive study of teachings with world renowned Masters, one of whom entrusted her with bringing the sacred Mudra techniques to the West. She is a Yoga College of India certified Yoga Therapist.

Sabrina holds a Bachelors Degree in Sensory Approaches to Healing, a Masters in Holistic Science, and a Doctorate in Ancient and Modern Approaches to Healing from the American Institute of Holistic Theology. She is board certified from the American Alternative medical Association and American Holistic Health Association.

She has been featured in media outlets such as The Los Angeles Times, CNBC News, Cosmopolitan, the cover of London Times Lifestyle, The Discovery Channel documentary on Hands, W magazine, First for Women, Health, Web- MD, Daily News, Focus, Yoga Journal, Australian Women's weekly, Blend, Daily Breeze, New Age, the Roseanne Show and various international live television programs. Her articles have been published in world-wide publications. She hosted her own weekly TV show educating about health, well-being and complementary medicine. She is an executive member of the World Yoga Council and has led numerous international Yoga Therapy educational programs. She directed and produced her interactive double DVD titled *Chakra Mudras* - a Visionary awards finalist. Sabrina also created award winning international Spa and Wellness Centers and is a motivational keynote conference speaker addressing large audiences all over the world.

She is the founder of MUDRA MASTERY ™ the world's only online Mudra Teacher and Mudra Therapy Education, Certification, and Mentorship program, with her certified graduates and therapists spreading these ancient teachings in over 26 countries around the world.

WWW.SABRINAMESKO.COM